DANNY PROULX'S Toolboxes & WORKBENCHES

POPULAR WOODWORKING BOOKS
CINCINNATI, OHIO
www.popularwoodworking.com

READ THIS IMPORTANT SAFETY NOTICE

To prevent accidents, keep safety in mind while you work. Use the safety guards installed on power equipment; they are for your protection. When working on power equipment, keep fingers away from saw blades, wear safety goggles to prevent injuries from flying wood chips and sawdust, wear headphones to protect your hearing and consider installing a dust vacuum to reduce the amount of airborne sawdust in your woodshop. Don't wear loose clothing, such as neckties or shirts with loose sleeves, or jewelry, such as rings, necklaces or bracelets, when working on power equipment. Tie back long hair to prevent it from getting caught in your equipment. People who are sensitive to certain chemicals should check the chemical content of any product before using it. The authors and editors who compiled this book have tried to make the contents as accurate and correct as possible. Plans, illustrations, photographs and text have been carefully checked. All instructions, plans and projects should be carefully read, studied and understood before beginning construction. In some photos, power tool guards have been removed to more clearly show the operation being demonstrated. Always use all safety guards and attachments that come with your power tools. Due to the variability of local conditions, construction materials, skill levels, etc., neither the author nor Popular Woodworking Books assumes any responsibility for any accidents, injuries, damages or other losses incurred as a result of the material presented in this book. Prices listed for supplies and equipment were current at the time of publication and are subject to change. Glass shelving should have all edges polished and must be tempered. Untempered glass shelves may shatter and can cause serious bodily injury. Tempered shelves are very strong and if they break will just crumble, minimizing personal injury.

METRIC CONVERSION CHART

to convert	*to*	*multiply by*
Inches	Centimeters	2.54
Centimeters	Inches	0.4
Feet	Centimeters	30.5
Centimeters	Feet	0.03
Yards	Meters	0.9
Meters	Yards	1.1
Sq. Inches	Sq. Centimeters	6.45
Sq. Centimeters	Sq. Inches	0.16
Sq. Feet	Sq. Meters	0.09
Sq. Meters	Sq. Feet	10.8
Sq. Yards	Sq. Meters	0.8
Sq. Meters	Sq. Yards	1.2
Pounds	Kilograms	0.45
Kilograms	Pounds	2.2
Ounces	Grams	28.4
Grams	Ounces	0.035

 Published by Popular Woodworking Books, an imprint of F+W Publications, Inc., 4700 East Galbraith Road, Cincinnati, Ohio, 45236. 800-289-0963. First edition.

Visit our Web site at www.popularwoodworking.com for information on more resources for woodworkers.

Other fine Popular Woodworking Books are available from your local bookstore or direct from the publisher.

10 09 08 07 06 6 5 4 3 2

Library of Congress Cataloging-in-Publication Data

Proulx, Danny, 1947-
Danny Proulx's toolboxes & workbenches.– 1st ed.
p. cm.
Includes index.
ISBN 13: 978-1-55870-707-8 (pbk.: alk. paper)
ISBN 10: 1-55870-707-7 (alk. paper)
1. Toolboxes–Design and construction. 2. Workbenches–Design and construction. 3. Cabinetwork. I. Title: Toolboxes & workbenches. II. Title: Danny Proulx's toolboxes and workbenches. III. Title.
TT197.5.T65P76 2004
684'.08–dc22

2004046097

ACQUISITIONS EDITOR: Jim Stack
EDITED BY: Jennifer Ziegler and Amy Hattersley
DESIGNED BY: Brian Roeth
PRODUCTION COORDINATED BY: Robin Richie
PAGE MAKEUP BY: Joni DeLuca
TECHNICAL DRAWINGS BY: Len Churchill of Lenmark Communications Ltd.
PHOTOGRAPHIC CONSULTANT: Michael Bowie, Lux Photographic Services
WORKSHOP SITE PROVIDED BY: Rideau Cabinets

ABOUT THE AUTHOR

Danny Proulx is the owner of Rideau Cabinets and is a contributing editor for *CabinetMaker* magazine. He also contributes freelance articles for *Canadian Woodworking, Canadian Home Workshop, Popular Woodworking* and other magazines. His earlier books include *Build Your Own Kitchen Cabinets, The Kitchen Cabinetmaker's Building and Business Manual, How to Build Classic Garden Furniture, Smart Shelving & Storage Solutions, Fast & Easy Techniques for Building Modern Cabinetry, Building More Classic Garden Furniture, Building Cabinet Doors & Drawers, Build Your Own Home Office Furniture, Display Cases You Can Build, Building Frameless Kitchen Cabinets, Building Woodshop Workstations* and *The Pocket Hole Drilling Jig Project Book.*

You can reach Danny via his Web site, www.cabinetmaking.com, and he can be reached by e-mail at danny@cabinetmaking.com.

TECHNICAL SUPPORT

I often turn to a number of companies for advice and supplies. They are always helpful and are a source of valuable information. They are major players in the creation of my books, and I've listed them in the back of this book under the heading of Suppliers. I'd appreciate your support of these fine companies.

ACKNOWLEDGEMENTS

This is another book of projects that I've enjoyed building, but I could never accomplish it alone. The people close to me are, as always, a big part of this book. My wife, Gale, is constantly helpful and supportive, as is my father-in-law and assistant, Jack Chaters.

Michael Bowie of Lux Photographic Services continues to show his amazing photographic talents and is the person I rely on for photographic expertise. He advises and guides me as I shoot the digital photos for each project. His desire to produce the best results and his expert advice contribute greatly to the final product.

Len Churchill of Lenmark Communications is the talented illustrator who has been working with me and producing the amazing project drawings. He is one of the best illustrators in the business and has an impressive understanding of the woodworking projects he's asked to draw.

As always, the Popular Woodworking Books staff continues to be unbelievably supportive. It's a team with great depth and knowledge, like editor Jim Stack, Jenny Ziegler, Amy Hattersley, Brian Roeth and so many others who are a part of every page in this book.

Luc Rousseau and Rick Beaulne are two talented woodworkers who have also been helpful in producing this book. They've helped with some of the building and other necessary, but not very glamorous, tasks around my shop. I appreciate their help.

And finally, thanks to two friends, Bernie Hopbach, owner of BSAC Automotive, and Hugh Smith, owner of the Village Cabinetmaker in Ottawa, Ontario, for letting me use their shops for a few of the pictures.

TABLE OF CONTENTS

INTRODUCTION
page 6

PROJECT ONE
toolbox tote
page 8

PROJECT TWO
simple workbench
page 14

PROJECT THREE
fold-away work center
page 22

PROJECT FOUR
rolling tool cabinet
page 32

PROJECT FIVE
tall storage cabinets
page 44

PROJECT SIX
simple sawhorses
page 52

PROJECT SEVEN
rolling shop cart
page 60

PROJECT EIGHT

hand tool wall cabinet

page 66

PROJECT NINE

base cabinet work center

page 74

PROJECT TEN

carpenter's toolbox

page 84

PROJECT ELEVEN

carver's tool chest

page 96

PROJECT TWELVE

mobile tool chest

page 106

PROJECT THIRTEEN

adjustable worktable

page 114

SUPPLIERS

page 126

INDEX

page 128

INTRODUCTION

I enjoy writing books for those I call "weekend warriors" — woodworkers who, like millions of people, have full-time jobs but love to get into the woodshop at every opportunity. Once again this book, like most of my others, is dedicated and directed to these special people.

Woodworkers often have to share their shop space with the family car or work in basement utility rooms. A few lucky people can afford the luxury of a large building dedicated to their hobby, but that isn't the norm. In most cases, tools and benches have to be stored away to make room for other family activities. That's fine, but the downside is the time lost to set up and put away all the tools and worktables. It can often take an hour to set up and another hour to tear down the shop, which means less time for the real projects.

I will try to cover a number of temporary-shop issues concerning tool storage, boxes and work centers that can be set up quickly and packed away just as fast. I'll also offer some suggestions and options with respect to security. The garage door isn't always locked, and that is a tempting situation for some less-than-honest people. Children also have easy access to garages, and we should be concerned about limiting access to potentially dangerous woodworking tools.

The toolbox tote is a must-have project for every woodworker who has to take a few tools along to family and friends when something needs fixing. This tote has a couple of nice features that make it quick to load as well as providing easy access to all types of tools.

The benches and work centers are built using standard dimension lumber that can be purchased at any wood supply store. The joinery is simple, effective and strong, so the projects should provide many years of service. They can be quickly taken apart and stored or folded up and locked.

I've come across a lot of great ideas that have been passed on to me by readers and woodworking club members. They all face the same storage and space restrictions, like most of us, and have devised unique solutions. For example, we all have six or eight small bench machines such as sanders, grinders, planers, joiners and so on. Dedicating workbench space for each one is often impossible, so we haul them out and spend time setting them up when needed. I built a rolling tool cabinet that can hold many of these small electric tools and provides a mobile worktop that can be used anywhere in the shop.

Woodworkers who enjoy carving and turning have a large number of handle tools that demand special storage. I'll show you a wall cabinet that might be just the answer to your storage requirements, or you might prefer the chest-style storage option in a later chapter.

If you have room for a fixed work and storage center, look at project nine. The base cabinet work center has a large work surface that's supported by storage cabinets so you can store all your important tools and get to them quickly when needed.

Project twelve deals with a situation that I face quite often. It's nice to go to family and friends and help build a deck, renovate a rec room, build a play center for the kids or dozens of other projects that demand your woodworking talents. However, your friends aren't woodworkers and don't have the tools you'll need for the project. That sometimes means loading the car trunk with electric and hand tools for the job. The mobile tool chest might just be the solution you're looking for when you get the call for help. It has plenty of room for all types of tools, the chest can be locked, and it has wheels and a handle that makes moving it a breeze.

Good luck building these projects. I'm sure you'll find three or four that will reduce the setup times in your shop and make woodworking a lot more enjoyable and productive. Please don't hesitate to change the dimensions to suit your requirements or use a different sheet material. Not every situation and solution is the same, so customize the projects and make them work for you.

toolbox tote

PROJECT 1

This easy-to-build toolbox tote is a must-have for any woodworker. It makes all those necessary home repairs a lot simpler because all your tools are close at hand. When friends or family call for help, all you have to do is load up the tote and you're on your way — no running back and forth for another handful of tools.

However, like my friend and editor Jim Stack of Popular Woodworking Books noted in his book *Building the Perfect Tool Chest,* small hand tools usually end up at the bottom of a tote box, making them hard to reach. Jim designed a unique holding system for screwdrivers along the box edges, so I wanted to see if I could also design a possible solution to the problem.

The bottom-mount tray feature is my answer to a small tool storage area that's easy to reach. Simply unlatch the draw catches, and the hand tool tray is released from the main box. All the small tools are clearly visible and easy to reach. The top section of the tote box can be used for levels and carpenter and combination squares, as well as a few small power tools.

This toolbox tote has everything within easy reach, so you don't need to fumble through a pile of tools to get a couple of screwdrivers hidden on the bottom of the box. As we all know, when tools are organized and easy to reach, the project always seems a lot easier. I think you'll find this tote design handy and also a pleasure to use.

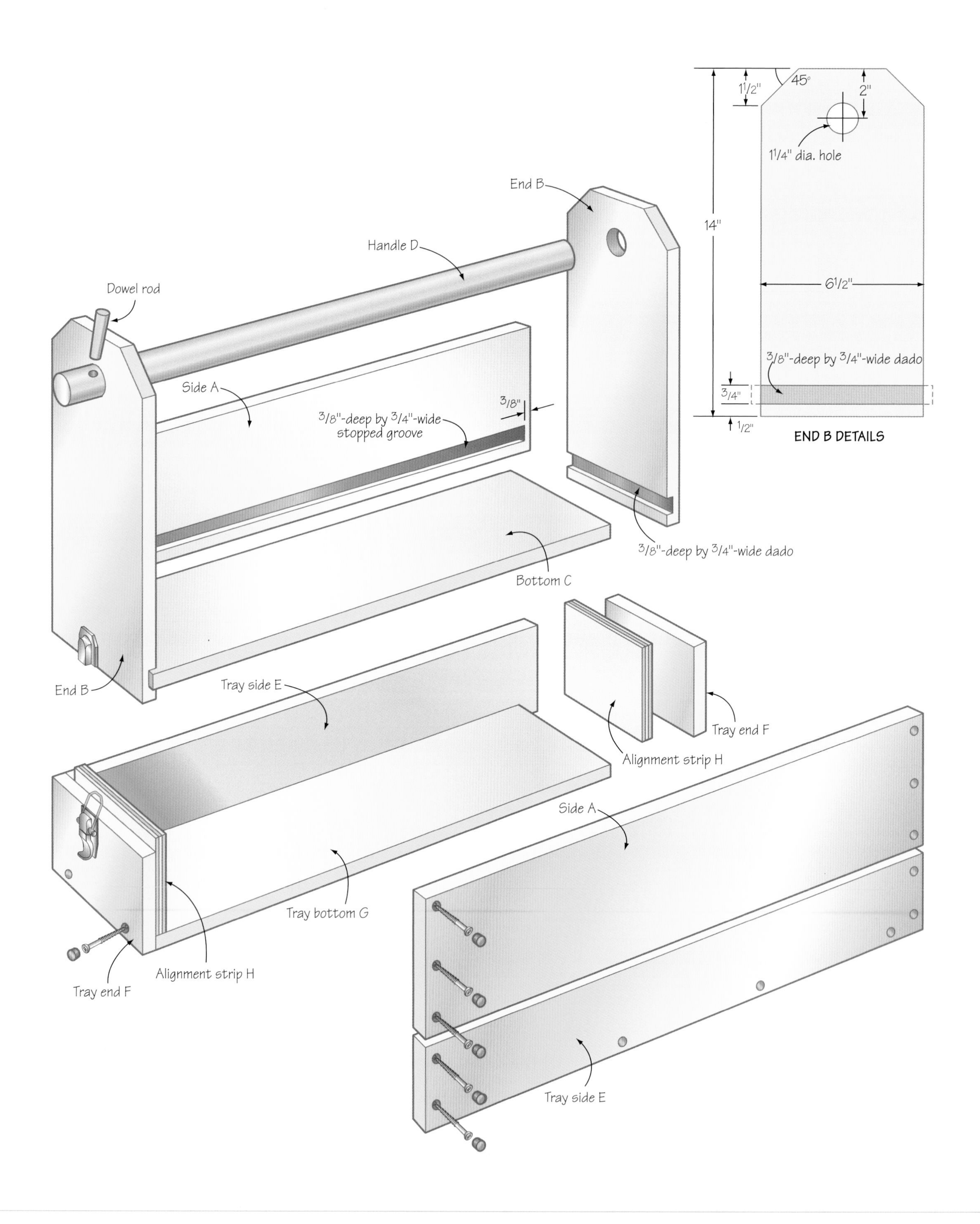
End B
Handle D
Dowel rod
Side A
3/8"
3/8"-deep by 3/4"-wide
stopped groove
Bottom C
3/8"-deep by 3/4"-wide dado
End B
Tray side E
Alignment strip H
Tray end F
Side A
Tray bottom G
Alignment strip H
Tray end F
Tray side E
45°
1 1/2"
2"
1 1/4" dia. hole
14"
6 1/2"
3/8"-deep by 3/4"-wide dado
3/4"
1/2"
END B DETAILS

inches (millimeters)

REFERENCE	QUANTITY	PART	STOCK	THICKNESS	(mm)	WIDTH	(mm)	LENGTH	(mm)
A	2	sides	pine	$^3/_4$	(19)	$7^1/_4$	(184)	28	(711)
B	2	ends	pine	$^3/_4$	(19)	$6^1/_2$	(165)	14	(356)
C	1	bottom	pine	$^3/_4$	(19)	$7^1/_4$	(184)	$27^1/_4$	(692)
D	1	handle	hardwood	$1^1/_4$ dia.	(32)			30	(762)
E	2	tray sides	pine	$^3/_4$	(19)	$3^1/_2$	(89)	28	(711)
F	2	tray ends	pine	$^3/_4$	(19)	$3^1/_2$	(89)	$6^1/_2$	(165)
G	1	tray bottom	pine	$^3/_4$	(19)	$6^1/_2$	(165)	$26^1/_2$	(673)
H	2	alignment strips	plywood	$^1/_2$	(13)	4	(102)	$6^1/_2$	(165)

hardware & supplies

	2" (51mm) screws
	nails
	glue
	$^5/_{16}$" (8mm) dowel pins
	mahogany wood plugs
2	draw catches

1 Cut the two sides A and two ends B to the sizes indicated in the materials list. The tops of both end panels B are mitered at 45°, $1^1/_2$" in from each side edge. Clamp the end panels together and ease the sharp corners with a sander. Since the ends are clamped, both will be formed equally and will be identical.

2 On the inside face of each end panel form a dado that's $^3/_4$" wide and $^1/_2$" above the bottom edge. Each side panel requires a $^3/_4$"- wide groove, $^1/_2$" above the bottom edge. All dadoes and grooves are $^3/_8$" deep. The grooves on the side boards should stop $^3/_8$" short of both ends. This technique is called a blind or stopped groove. The grooves and dadoes can be formed with a router mounted in a table or on a table saw using a dado blade. There are a number of cutting options, but be sure to square the ends of all the cuts to properly fit the bottom board.

SHOP *tip*

If you can't fully hide a joint, celebrate it, as one longtime cabinetmaker said. To do this I'm using dark mahogany plugs, which are a nice contrast to the light pine boards.

3 I am using a 1¼"-diameter hardwood dowel rod for my tote box handle D. The dowel will pass through drilled holes near the top edge of each end B. Drill the 1¼"-diameter holes centered on each end panel and located 2" on center below the top edge. Clamp both panels together and drill the holes. Use a piece of scrap lumber under the boards to prevent wood tear-out.

4 The bottom C is installed in the grooves and dadoes. To allow the wood to expand and contract, don't use glue to secure the bottom. Assemble the tote box and clamp tightly when all the parts are aligned.

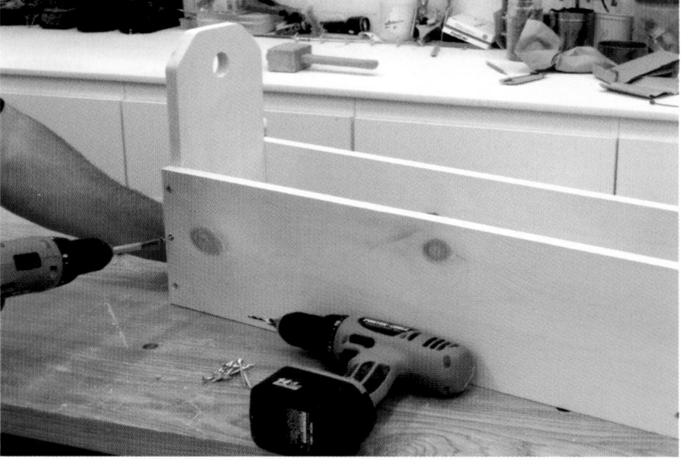

5 Use three 2"-long screws to secure each corner joint. Counterbore the screw holes, using a ⅜"-diameter counterbore drill bit.

6 Cut a 1¼"-diameter dowel rod 30" long to create handle D. Drill two 5⁄16"-diameter holes through the rod, ¾" on center from each end. Thread the dowel rod through the previously drilled holes in the end boards and drive 2"-long, 5⁄16"-diameter dowel pins into the holes on the handle. Use a little glue on each dowel pin, being careful not to glue the dowel rod to the end boards. The tote box will be much easier to lift and carry if the handle rotates freely.

7 The tool tray is built with the two tray sides E, two tray ends F and the tray bottom board G. Secure the sides and end boards to the bottom board. Use a little glue and 2" screws in counterbored holes. Fill the holes with mahogany wood plugs. The tray should have the same outside dimensions as the tote box section.

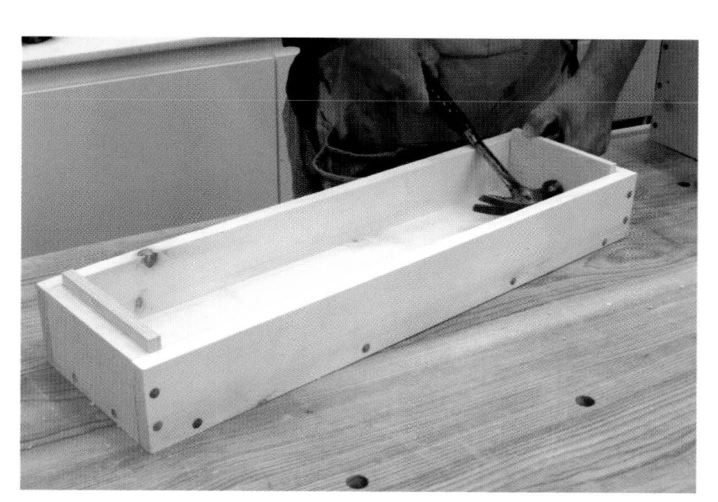

8 Use two ½"-thick by 4"-high pieces of plywood to form the alignment strips H. The strips are glued and nailed in place on each end board. These strips will align the main box to the tray.

9 Install two draw catches, one on each end of the box, to secure the tray to the main box. Note that the tongue on the top section of each catch should be aligned with the bottom edge of the tote box. If the tongues were below the bottom of the end panel, they might scratch the floor when the tray is removed.

construction NOTES

Apply a finish to the box to complete the project. I used three coats of polyurethane to protect the wood.

This project was built using pine, but just about any solid wood or sheet material will work as well. A solid hardwood box will be more resistant to bumps and dents than this pine box, so if you want that type of durability, use hardwood. Sheet materials, such as ¾"-thick plywood, would also be very strong. Multicore materials such as plywood do not expand and contract as much as solid wood, so all the joints can be glued to strengthen the tote.

You may have specific tool carrying needs, so change the sizes to suit your requirements. If you carry a lot of hand tools, the upper section can be downsized and the tray built deeper. Wood pegs could be added to one side of the box to wrap extension cords that are often needed on the job, or divider slots can be installed in the upper section to keep your tools separated. The options are endless with this great little carrying box.

simple workbench

PROJECT 2

A workbench in any woodshop is a necessary item. Most benches are the center of activity in the workroom and one of your most important tools. However, if you share your work space with the family car in the garage,or with the pool table in the basement activity room, or if you must work in the backyard, having a good sturdy bench isn't always possible.

How would you like a strong bench, with an accessory shelf, that can be assembled in minutes or taken apart just as quickly for storage? What about having all bench parts bolted together when stored so you'll be able to find everything quickly? This simple workbench project may be just what you need — sturdy, easy to put together, quick to take apart and suitable for any of your woodworking projects.

This simple workbench can be built for less than $80, using one ¾"-thick sheet of plywood, a half sheet of hardboard, a few feet of hardwood for the tabletop trim and three 8' lengths of framing lumber. It's extremely sturdy and can be built in one evening in your workshop with a few simple electric tools. In fact, if your local lumberyard can cut the plywood sheet to size, half the work will be done.

I've built this bench with hardware so the shelf and leg assemblies can be easily taken apart. But you can use glue and screws, as I will detail in the construction notes, if you don't need to take the bench apart. The top is 1¾" thick, perfectly flat and strong enough to hold any project in progress.

The fold-flat storage feature is important to many woodworkers who share their work space, but a contractor friend of mine mentioned another use that I hadn't considered. He is going to build the bench and use it for on-site work where a strong worktable is a real bonus. He also said this bench design would be handy for any woodworker who helps family and friends with their renovation projects. Maybe this should be called the traveling workbench project.

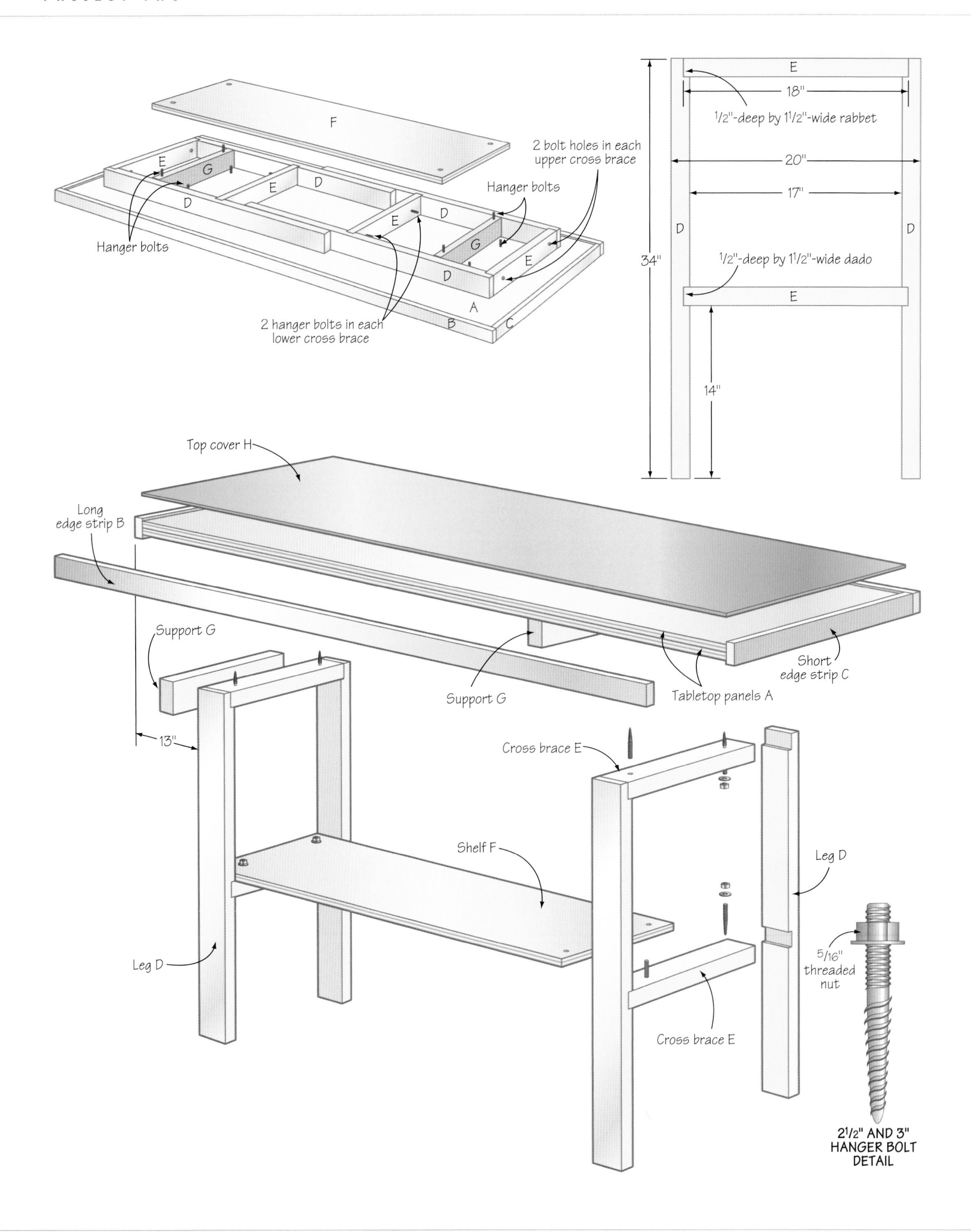
F
E
G
E
D
D
E
D
G
E
D
A
B
C
Hanger bolts
Hanger bolts
2 bolt holes in each
upper cross brace
2 hanger bolts in each
lower cross brace
E
18"
1/2"-deep by 1 1/2"-wide rabbet
20"
17"
D
D
34"
1/2"-deep by 1 1/2"-wide dado
E
14"
Top cover H
Long
edge strip B
Support G
Support G
Tabletop panels A
Short
edge strip C
13"
Cross brace E
Shelf F
Leg D
Leg D
Cross brace E
5/16" threaded nut
2 1/2" AND 3"
HANGER BOLT
DETAIL

inches (millimeters)

REFERENCE	QUANTITY	PART	STOCK	THICKNESS	(mm)	WIDTH	(mm)	LENGTH	(mm)
A	2	tabletop panels	plywood	3/4	(19)	23 15/16	(608)	72	(1829)
B	2	long edge strips	hardwood	3/4	(19)	1 3/4	(45)	73 1/2	(1867)
C	2	short edge strips	hardwood	3/4	(19)	1 3/4	(45)	23 15/16	(608)
D	4	legs	softwood	1 1/2	(38)	3 1/2	(89)	34	(864)
E	4	cross braces	softwood	1 1/2	(38)	3 1/2	(89)	18	(457)
F	1	shelf	plywood	3/4	(19)	17	(432)	48	(1219)
G	2	supports	softwood	1 1/2	(38)	3 1/2	(89)	17	(432)
H	1	top cover	hardboard	1/4	(6)	23 15/16	(608)	72	(1829)

hardware & supplies

nails
glue
2" (51mm) screws
8 5/16" x 2 1/2" (8mm x 64mm) hanger bolts
4 5/16" x 3" (8mm x 76mm) hanger bolts
12 5/16" (8mm) washers
12 5/16" (8mm) nuts

1 Prepare the two tabletop plywood panels A for the workbench top. The first cut, to optimize the 4' x 8' sheet, should be a crosscut along the width so you'll have one panel at 48" x 72" and one shorter panel at 48" wide. The shorter panel will be used for the bench shelf later in the project. Rip the longer panel into two equal sheets that are approximately 23 5/16" wide by 72" long. The kerf (thickness) of your blade will determine the final width after cutting the sheets; however, most blades are about 1/8" thick. If you don't have a table saw capable of cutting the large panels, use a circular saw or have the lumberyard cut the panels to size.

2 Use glue to bond the two sheets together, creating a top that's 1 1/2" thick by 23 15/16" wide by 72" long. Hold the sheets in alignment with a few small nails and place weight on the panel until the adhesive sets.

3 The workbench top will have a cover made of hardboard, sometimes called Masonite, that's available in a number of thicknesses. Measure the thickness of the sandwiched plywood panel and the hardboard cover. I'm using $\frac{1}{4}$" hardboard for my cover, so the total top thickness is $1\frac{3}{4}$". Cut the two long edge strips B and two short edge strips C to the sizes indicated in the materials list, or to the correct size for your table if your top dimensions are different from mine. Mount the strips flush with the bottom face of the plywood panel so they will be $\frac{1}{4}$" above the top surface. This lip rising above the surface will hold the hardboard cover in place. Secure the edge strips with glue and 2" screws (or biscuit joinery if you have the tools and want to hide the edge fasteners). Small finishing nails and glue can also be used to hold the strips. The joinery technique doesn't matter as long as you are satisfied with the appearance.

SHOP *tip*

If you don't own a router table or dado blade set for your table saw, you can make rabbets and dadoes with a circular saw. Draw cut lines on the lumber, set the saw blade depth to $\frac{1}{2}$", and make a series of kerf cuts within the lines for each rabbet or dado. Break the small pieces with a chisel and hammer, then clean the joint with a sharp chisel.

4 The leg assemblies are made with 2x4 framing lumber. Cut parts D and E to the lengths stated and form the dadoes and rabbets on the four legs D. All dadoes and rabbets are $\frac{1}{2}$" deep by $1\frac{1}{2}$" wide and located as shown in the illustration.

5 Build the two leg assemblies by first putting glue in the rabbets and dadoes. Join the cross braces E and legs D as shown and drive 2" screws in pilot holes through the leg into each cross brace. Two screws per joint, along with the glue, will create a strong bond. Remember to drill pilot holes for the screws to avoid splitting the soft lumber.

6 Draw position lines across the underside of the tabletop that are 13" from each end. Measure and draw cross lines (about 2$^{11}/_{16}$") from each table side to position each leg assembly on the center of the workbench top.

7 Position the leg assemblies and drill two $^{3}/_{16}$"-diameter holes through each upper brace into the workbench top. Drill 1" into the plywood panels. Set the leg assemblies aside, then in the workbench top, thread the coarse end of a 3"-long by $^{5}/_{16}$"-diameter hanger bolt into each hole, leaving 2" of the bolt exposed. Enlarge the through-holes in both braces so the leg assemblies will fit over the shafts of the $^{5}/_{16}$" bolts . Secure the legs with washers and nuts.

SHOP *tip*

Many woodworking stores carry a large selection of threaded hanger bolts and knobs. You can use these knobs in place of the nuts for quicker assembly.

8 Once both leg assemblies have been securely fastened, turn the workbench right-side up. Cut the shelf F to size using the offcut from the plywood sheet. Drill two $^{3}/_{16}$"-diameter holes through each end of the shelf into the lower braces. Drill $1^{1}/_{4}$" into each brace. Secure the shelf panel to the lower braces using $^{5}/_{16}$" by $2^{1}/_{2}$"-long hanger bolts, washers and nuts.

9 If your bench will be used in a fixed position all the time (see the construction notes), proceed to step 11. Otherwise, remove the shelf and leg assemblies that are attached to the workbench top. Lay the legs on the bottom face of the top as shown. Next, cut two 17" lengths of 2x4s to create the supports G. Align the supports on the bench top so that the existing mounting holes in the shelf can be centered on each support, but be sure the supports don't cover the areas where the leg assemblies get attached to the bench top. Secure the supports with glue and two 2" screws driven through the top side of the workbench.

10 Use the shelf as a template to position hanger bolts in each support. Install $5/16$"-diameter by $2^1/2$"-long hanger bolts in each support. Put the shelf on the supports, with the legs lying flat, and secure the shelf board to the supports with nuts and washers. Tighten the nuts and test the folded-up position of your workbench.

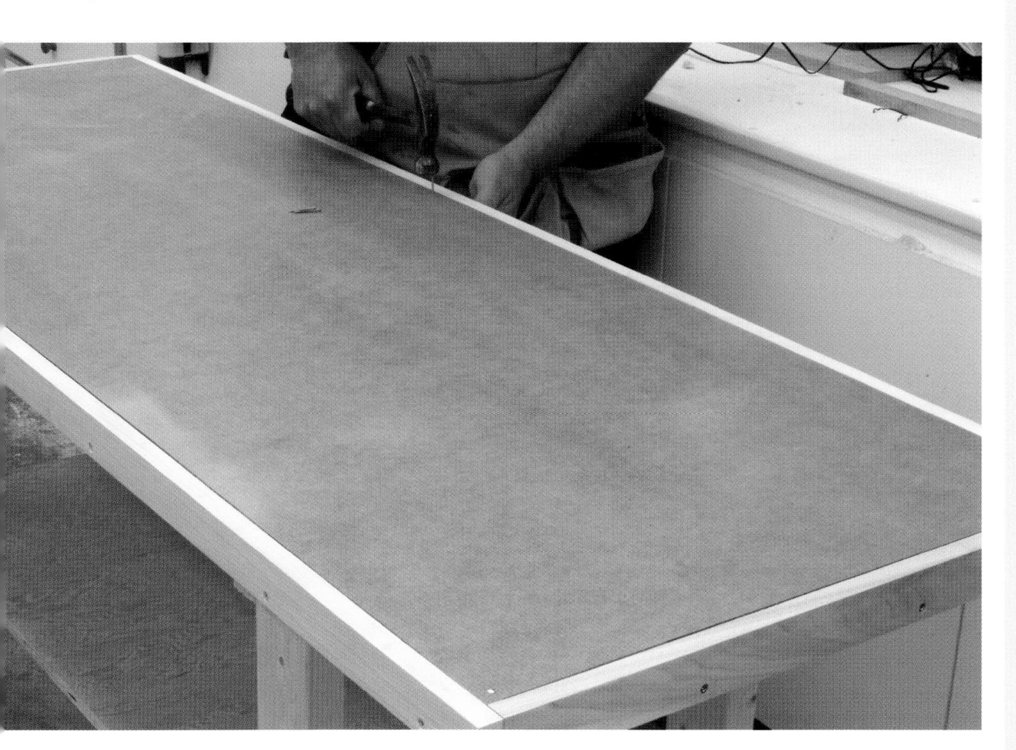

11 Cut the $1/4$"-thick hardboard top cover H to size. Secure the cover with a few small nails. These nails can be easily removed if the top needs replacing.

construction NOTES

The first decision you should make before building the workbench concerns its use. Do you want it assembled all the time? Will you use the fold-up feature? If you don't need to store the bench flat, replace the hanger bolts and nuts with glue and 2" screws to permanently secure the legs and shelf.

However, having the option to pack the bench flat could be a valuable asset if it needs to be transported for a move or taken to a work site. If you live in temporary quarters, share your woodworking space with the family car or work at woodworking projects only occasionally, the storage option might be worth considering.

I built the bench using $1/4$" G1S (good one side) plywood and construction-grade 2x4 lumber. You could use a less expensive sheet material like $3/4$" medium-density fiberboard (MDF) or particleboard to lower the cost. The legs could be made from hardwood, which is a little more resistant to damage, but that's a lot more costly than construction-grade softwood. The edge around the workbench top should be a hardwood, as that area will suffer a lot of bumps and scrapes. If you want to keep the cost as low as possible because you use the bench only three or four times each year, build it with construction-grade lumber and MDF sheet stock.

The bench can be protected with good oil-based paint. And if the floor in your work space is uneven, install adjustable feet or levelers on each leg. Adjustable feet are available at hardware stores and are usually installed in drilled holes in the leg bottoms. They provide about $3/4$" adjustment, which should be sufficient for most garage floors.

fold-away work center

PROJECT 3

This project is all about secure storage and a solid worktable that sets up quickly — but it's also about cost. This work center, with a solid table and lockable storage for tools and supplies, can be built for $75 or less.

I used two sheets of ¾"-thick medium-density fiberboard (MDF) to build the cabinet and bench. However, if you're not fond of MDF, you can use any sheet material. The real plus with MDF is its low cost; the downside is its weight. The worktable weighs nearly 100 pounds, so that might be a consideration. The two-layer MDF worktable sandwich is flat, stable and sturdy, but you'll have to use a little extra caution when lifting it into a horizontal position. Plywood is quite a bit lighter, but it's also a lot more expensive. I like MDF for workshop cabinets because of the low cost, smooth work surface and weight, which tends to stabilize tables and cabinetry.

The table drops almost flat against a wall, and the folding cabinet is only 8" deep when closed. Tool and material storage is right above the workbench for quick access. When you're ready to work on a project, open the wings of the locked cabinet, raise the bench and lock the supports, install the cross brace and you're set to go. You will be able to set up and break down the center in less than two minutes. No time is wasted dragging tables around the garage or looking for tools.

My favorite feature is the security provided by this project. Valuable and sometimes dangerous tools or equipment can be locked in a cabinet that only you can open. A garage workshop isn't the most secure place, because children can get at sharp chisels or supplies they shouldn't be handling. Well-meaning neighbors sometimes borrow tools that are lying around the garage, and items often have a habit of disappearing. This fold-away work center eliminates these problems and ensures that your tools and supplies are always where you left them.

I'm sure you'll find this project useful in a shop where you share space. It's easy and inexpensive to build. Once it's installed, move the car outside and you'll be ready to work wood in a couple of minutes!

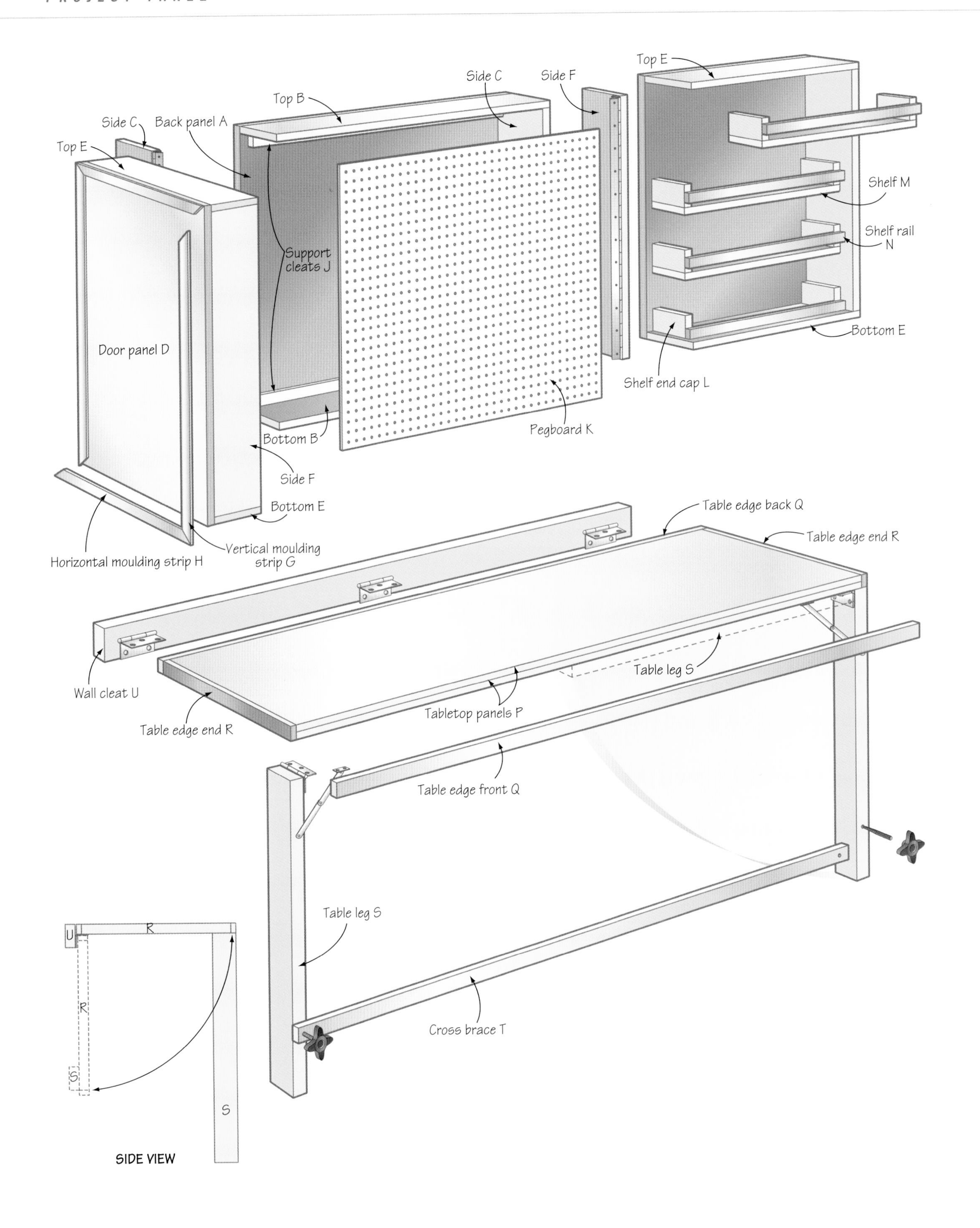
Top E
Side C
Back panel A
Top B
Side C
Side F
Top E
Shelf M
Shelf rail N
Support cleats J
Door panel D
Bottom B
Pegboard K
Bottom E
Shelf end cap L
Side F
Bottom E
Horizontal moulding strip H
Vertical moulding strip G
Table edge back Q
Table edge end R
Wall cleat U
Table leg S
Tabletop panels P
Table edge end R
Table edge front Q
Table leg S
Cross brace T
U
R
R
S
S
SIDE VIEW

inches (millimeters)

REFERENCE	QUANTITY	PART	STOCK	THICKNESS	(mm)	WIDTH	(mm)	LENGTH	(mm)
A	1	back panel	MDF	$\frac{3}{4}$	(19)	30	(762)	36	(914)
B	2	top and bottom	MDF	$\frac{3}{4}$	(19)	4	(102)	36	(914)
C	2	sides	MDF	$\frac{3}{4}$	(19)	4	(102)	$28\frac{1}{2}$	(724)
D	2	door panels	MDF	$\frac{3}{4}$	(19)	30	(762)	$17\frac{15}{16}$	(456)
E	4	top and bottom	MDF	$\frac{3}{4}$	(19)	4	(102)	$17\frac{15}{16}$	(456)
F	4	sides	MDF	$\frac{3}{4}$	(19)	4	(102)	$28\frac{1}{2}$	(724)
G	4	vertical moulding strips	pine	$\frac{1}{4}$	(6)	$1\frac{1}{4}$	(32)	30	(762)
H	4	horizontal moulding strips	pine	$\frac{1}{4}$	(6)	$1\frac{1}{4}$	(32)	18	(457)
J	2	support cleats	plywood	$\frac{1}{2}$	(13)	1	(25)	$34\frac{1}{2}$	(876)
K	1	pegboard panel	hardboard	$\frac{1}{4}$	(6)	$28\frac{1}{2}$	(724)	$34\frac{1}{2}$	(876)
L	16	shelf end caps	MDF	$\frac{3}{4}$	(19)	$3\frac{1}{2}$	(89)	$3\frac{1}{2}$	(89)
M	6	shelf boards	MDF	$\frac{3}{4}$	(19)	$3\frac{1}{2}$	(89)	$16\frac{1}{2}$	(419)
N	8	shelf rails	pine	$\frac{1}{4}$	(6)	$1\frac{1}{4}$	(32)	$16\frac{1}{2}$	(419)
P	2	tabletop panels	MDF	$\frac{3}{4}$	(19)	24	(610)	$70\frac{1}{2}$	(1791)
Q	2	table edges front and back	hardwood	$\frac{3}{4}$	(19)	$1\frac{1}{2}$	(38)	72	(1829)
R	2	table end edges	hardwood	$\frac{3}{4}$	(19)	$1\frac{1}{2}$	(38)	24	(610)
S	2	table legs	pine	$1\frac{1}{2}$	(38)	$3\frac{1}{2}$	(89)	$34\frac{1}{2}$	(876)
T	1	cross brace	hardwood	$\frac{3}{4}$	(19)	$1\frac{1}{2}$	(38)	72	(1829)
U	1	wall cleat	pine	$1\frac{1}{2}$	(38)	$3\frac{1}{2}$	(89)	72	(1829)

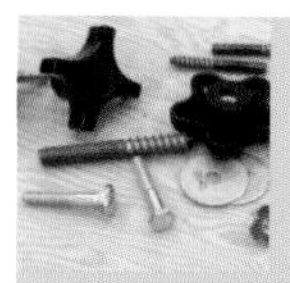

hardware & supplies

- $\frac{5}{8}$" (16mm) or $\frac{3}{4}$" (19mm) coarse-threaded screws
- $1\frac{1}{4}$" (32mm) screws
- $1\frac{1}{2}$" (38mm) screws
- 3" (76mm) wood screws
- glue
- 2 30" (762mm) piano hinges
- brad nails
- decorative washers
- barrel bolt
- bolt latch
- lock hasp
- wood plugs

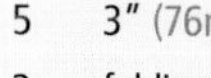

- 5 3" (76mm) butt hinges
- 2 folding supports
- 2 $2\frac{1}{2}$" (64mm) hanger bolts
- 2 threaded knobs

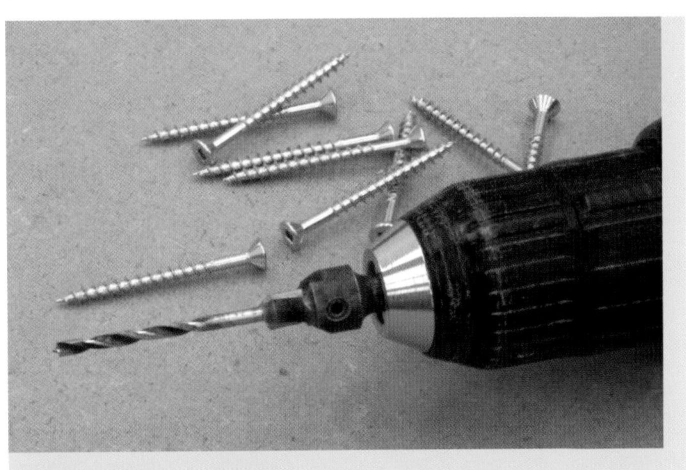

SHOP *tip*

MDF can easily split when driving screws. Here are a couple of tips to minimize damage to the board. First, always predrill screw holes before driving screws into the boards. To further eliminate splits, extend the drill bit so the pilot hole will be at least 1/8" longer than the screw shaft. Finally, stay at least 1" away from board ends when installing screws.

1 Cut the back panel A as well as the top and bottom B and sides C to the sizes indicated in the materials list. The four panels B and C are attached to the back panel A with glue and 1½"-long screws as shown in the illustration. These four panels are aligned with the outside edges of the back panel. Drive screws through the rear face of the back panel into the B and C panel edges, spacing them about 6" apart, but first be sure to drill pilot holes in the MDF. Glue and a screw should also be used at each corner where the side, top and bottom boards meet. If you have a plate joiner and prefer biscuits instead of screws, use No. 20s to join the panels, but you'll have to clamp all the joints until the adhesive sets. Remember, screws will not be seen on the rear face of panel A after the cabinet is installed.

2 Build two doors following the same assembly procedure as in step 1, using panels D, E and F. Each door width is 1/16" narrower than one-half the total cabinet width. That dimension will provide a 1/8" gap between the doors when mounted. Use glue and 1½" screws in pilot holes to build the wing doors.

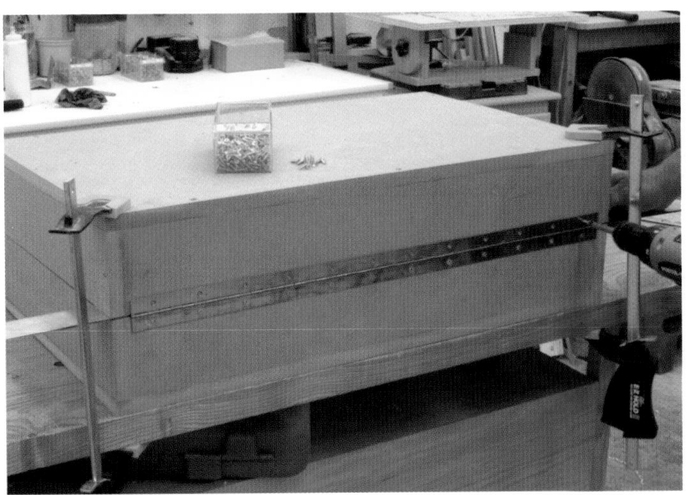

3 Attach each door case to the backboard case using a 28"-or 30"-long piano hinge. I've installed the hinges on the outside face of each box instead of the normal inside edge. An MDF edge will not offer as much hold for the screws as the panel face, so I decided this was a better method for hinge installation. While you install the hinges, temporarily place a 1/16" spacer between the backboard and wing doors so the doors will operate without binding. Use a 5/8"- or 3/4"-long coarse-threaded screw to secure the hinges, filling each hinge hole with a screw.

4 Install moulding strips G and H on both front panels D of the swing doors. I used a standard lumber supply moulding called Parclose, which is readily available. Use glue and brad nails to attach the moulding, joining the corners with 45° miters. The moulding is not a necessary structural item; however, the moulding hides screw heads and adds a little visual interest to the case.

5 You can configure the inside of the wall case in a number of ways. The interior shelves and tool holders should be designed to meet your requirements. I'll detail one possible design that you may find useful. First, install two support cleats J, which will support the $^1/_4$" pegboard in the center section. These cleats are installed at the top and bottom of the case to provide space for the hangers to poke out behind the pegboard. Use any $^1/_2$"-thick stock that you have lying around the shop, as the cleats will not be visible. Glue and a few brad nails will secure the cleats.

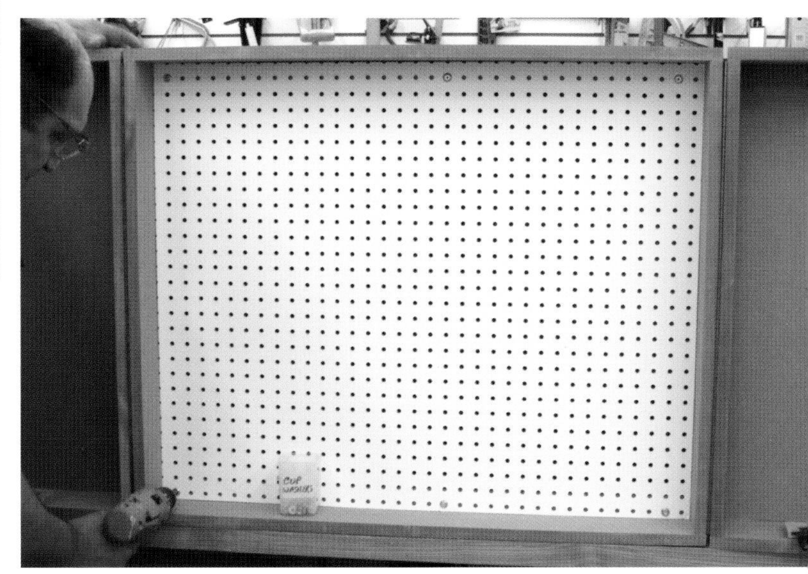

6 Attach a pegboard panel K to the cleats with $1^1/_4$"-long screws and decorative washers. Three screws in the top and bottom cleat will secure the panel.

7 I'm installing shelves in each door. They are made using $^3/_4$"-thick MDF and strips of Parclose moulding. The shelves are built using the end caps L and shelf boards M. The rails N keep the materials and supplies from falling off the shelves. Each assembly is attached to the door sides with one screw. I didn't use glue so that I can move the shelves in case my storage requirements change. The moulding rails are attached with glue and brad nails. The bottom rack or shelf assembly doesn't require a shelf board.

8 Install a barrel bolt on the inside of one door. It will secure the door and prevent movement when a latch and lock is installed. Attach a small square of wood with glue and $1^1/_2$" screws on the door's inside edge to mount the bolt assembly. Close the door, mark where the slide bolt touches the cabinet's bottom board and drill a hole for the barrel.

9 Attach a lock hasp assembly to the doors. You may have to chisel and form the perimeter moulding to mount the hasp. Buy the hardware, hold it in place and mark its position. A little trimming of the moulding should be all that's needed to mount the latch.

10 Cut the two tabletop panels P to create a 1½"-thick workbench top. Put standard white or yellow glue on the face of one panel and then lay the other on top, being sure to align the edges. Clamp the panel sandwich and drive 1¼" screws into the bottom face to hold the panels together until the glue sets properly.

SHOP *tip*

You will get both workbench top panels from one sheet of MDF. It typically comes in sheets that measure 49" by 97", so there should be plenty of material for the saw kerf (width of the blade cut in material). Be careful handling ¾" MDF because a full sheet weighs almost 100 pounds and the workbench top sandwich is a full sheet. Get some help to move it around if necessary.

11 Attach the four hardwood edge strips Q and R to the MDF panels. I attached my hardwood edges with glue and 1½" screws in ⅜"-diameter counterbored holes. After the screws were installed, I filled the holes with wood plugs. You can also attach the edge strips with biscuits, dowels, splines or by simply gluing and clamping. Use whichever method makes you most comfortable.

12 The top surface of my workbench top will be 36" high because I find that height comfortable. The leg heights can be changed to suit your height preference. Cut the two legs S to the size shown in the materials list. Use 3" butt hinges to attach the legs to the underside of the workbench top, as shown, at each end. Test the folded position of the legs, making sure they lie flat and do not contact each other.

13 Purchase and install folding supports for each leg. In many cases, there are right- and left-side supports, so check the package labels when you buy the hardware. Install the supports following the manufacturer's instructions.

14 To increase the stability of the legs, install the cross brace T. The brace is attached to each leg with hanger bolts and threaded knobs for quick installation and removal. Use $2^1/_2$"-long threaded hanger bolts and the proper knobs. Drill holes at each end of the cross brace for the hanger bolts. Locate the rail near the middle of each leg.

SHOP *tip*

When all the leg and wall cleat hardware is attached, the table underside should look as shown in the photograph. Once the table is mounted on the wall, the underside will not be visible, or easily accessible, so be sure the legs and wall cleat operate properly.

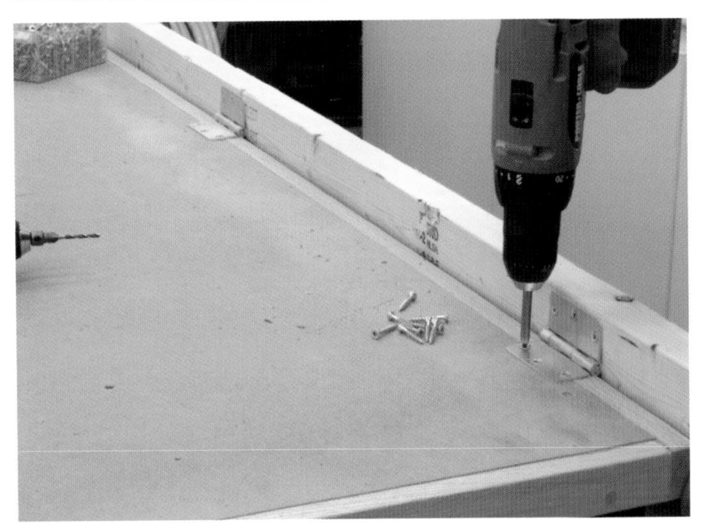

15 The workbench will be supported on the wall by a cleat. This wall cleat U is a 6' length of construction-grade framing lumber. The table is attached to the wall cleat using 3" butt hinges and $1^1/_4$"-long screws. The wall cleat's top edge, when attached to the wall, is aligned flush with the top surface of the workbench top.

16 Secure the wall cabinet to any wall by driving 3" screws through the pegboard and into the wall studs 12" to 18" above the bench top surface. Be sure the cabinet is level and plumb. The wall cleat U is attached to wall studs with 3" wood screws. The top edge of the cleat will be level and set at 36" above the floor.

SHOP *tip*

If your garage or basement floor is uneven, as mine is, install adjustable feet on the table legs. The feet are available at hardware stores. Or you could vary each leg length to match your floor based on a level tabletop. Another simple method would be to cut a block to the correct thickness to shim the leg.

construction NOTES

As I often mention in these construction notes, material choice is a secondary issue. If you'd prefer to work with plywood instead of MDF, don't hesitate. Material choice is a matter of personal preference, so use what you are most comfortable working with and what is right for the conditions. For example, some garage workshops are damp and subject to water leaks, so I'd consider a water-resistant sheet material or at least one that I could paint to offer added protection.

The wall cabinet size should also be modified to suit your needs. You may want to store expensive power tools or small hand tools, so build the cabinet to meet those requirements. Each door wing is normally one-half the back cabinet width, less 1⁄16". It's easy to calculate the panel measurements for a 40"-wide cabinet with two 19 15⁄16" doors, and so on.

The wall cabinet height above the workbench is usually in the 12" to 18" range, but that's not a fixed rule. Your woodworking interests may require more space between the bench top and cabinet, so raise it to the height you need.

Finally, there's the issue of bench height. I know of no rule that demands a specific height. The leg length can be any height to meet the needs of someone short or tall. You might want to use a stool at the bench if you do a lot of woodcarving or scroll sawing. If that's the case, remember the rule of 12s, which states the stool seat height should be 12" less than the bench top surface height. A 36"-high bench top would require a 24"-high stool, and so on.

rolling tool cabinet

PROJECT 4

Some might say this cabinet project is a bit fancy for a shop tool cabinet. That's probably a true statement, but I have good reasons for building this frame and panel cabinet with oak. First, I had a lot of cutoff pieces in my shop, and this cabinetmaking style is the perfect way to use wood shorts. Second, and more importantly, I wanted to fully detail this building style for those who have never used frame and panel construction techniques.

This cabinetmaking style isn't just for shop cabinets; it can be used for a whole variety of projects in your home. Living room furniture, bedroom suites, sideboards, entertainment center cabinets and so on — it's an endless list. Before modern sheet goods became popular, frame and panel construction methods were widely used. You can easily build structural panels, doors, drawer faces or mirror frames once you understand this woodworking construction style.

I'll detail some of the other project options for the frame and panel style in the construction notes. However, look closely at the procedures used to create individual panels. That's the heart of this construction method — grooves and tenons. It sounds a bit complicated, but all that's involved is making basic saw cuts using a table saw. That's it! You can build all the panels and doors you need with your table saw and careful cutting. In fact, you don't even have to change the blade.

However, before you decide to tackle a house full of frame and panel cabinetry, build yourself this rolling tool cabinet. It's a great way to practice all the techniques, and you wind up with a useful and versatile shop cabinet.

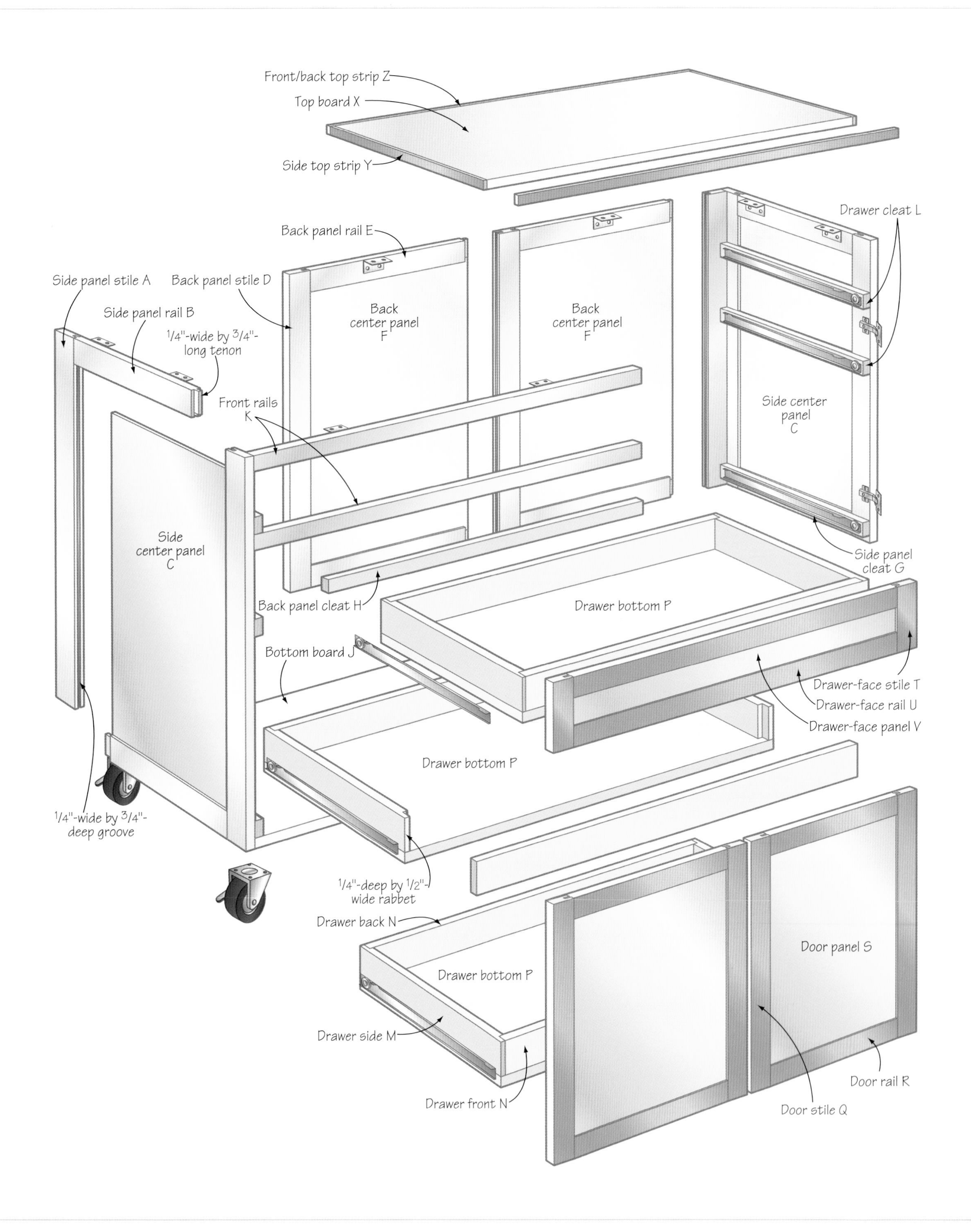

Front/back top strip Z
Top board X
Side top strip Y
Back panel rail E
Drawer cleat L
Side panel stile A
Back panel stile D
Side panel rail B
Back center panel F
Back center panel F
1/4"-wide by 3/4"-long tenon
Front rails K
Side center panel C
Side center panel C
Side panel cleat G
Back panel cleat H
Drawer bottom P
Bottom board J
Drawer-face stile T
Drawer-face rail U
Drawer-face panel V
Drawer bottom P
1/4"-wide by 3/4"-deep groove
1/4"-deep by 1/2"-wide rabbet
Drawer back N
Door panel S
Drawer bottom P
Drawer side M
Door rail R
Drawer front N
Door stile Q

inches (millimeters)

REFERENCE	QUANTITY	PART	STOCK	THICKNESS	(mm)	WIDTH	(mm)	LENGTH	(mm)
A	4	side panel stiles	hardwood	3/4	(19)	2 1/8	(54)	31	(787)
B	4	side panel rails	hardwood	3/4	(19)	2 1/8	(54)	17 1/4	(438)
C	2	side center panels	plywood	1/4	(6)	17 1/4	(438)	28 1/4	(718)
D	3	back panel stiles	hardwood	3/4	(19)	2 1/8	(54)	31	(787)
E	4	back panel rails	hardwood	3/4	(19)	2 1/8	(54)	16 5/16	(414)
F	2	back center panels	plywood	1/4	(6)	16 5/16	(414)	28 1/4	(718)
G	2	side panel cleats	hardwood	3/4	(19)	1 1/2	(38)	18 1/2	(470)
H	1	back panel cleat	hardwood	3/4	(19)	1 1/2	(38)	36	(914)
J	1	bottom board	plywood	3/4	(19)	19 1/4	(489)	36	(914)
K	2	front rails	hardwood	3/4	(19)	1 1/2	(38)	36	(914)
L	4	drawer cleats	hardwood	3/4	(19)	1 1/2	(38)	19	(483)
M	6	drawer sides	plywood	1/2	(13)	3 1/2	(89)	18	(457)
N	6	drawer fronts and backs	plywood	1/2	(13)	3 1/2	(89)	33	(838)
P	3	drawer bottoms	plywood	1/2	(13)	18	(457)	33 1/2	(851)
Q	4	door stiles	hardwood	3/4	(19)	2 1/8	(54)	23 1/2	(597)
R	4	door rails	hardwood	3/4	(19)	2 1/8	(54)	15 3/4	(400)
S	2	door panels	plywood	1/4	(6)	15 3/4	(400)	20 3/4	(527)
T	2	drawer-face stiles	hardwood	3/4	(19)	2 1/8	(54)	6	(152)
U	2	drawer-face rails	hardwood	3/4	(19)	2 1/8	(54)	34 1/4	(870)
V	1	drawer-face panel	plywood	1/4	(6)	3 1/4	(83)	34 1/4	(870)
W	1	drawer-face filler	plywood	1/4	(6)	1 3/4	(45)	30	(762)
X	1	top board	plywood	3/4	(19)	23	(584)	39	(991)
Y	2	side top strips	hardwood	1/4	(6)	3/4	(19)	23	(584)
Z	2	front/back top strips	hardwood	1/4	(6)	3/4	(19)	39 1/2	(1003)
AA	1	bottom strip	hardwood	1/4	(6)	3/4	(19)	39 1/2	(1003)

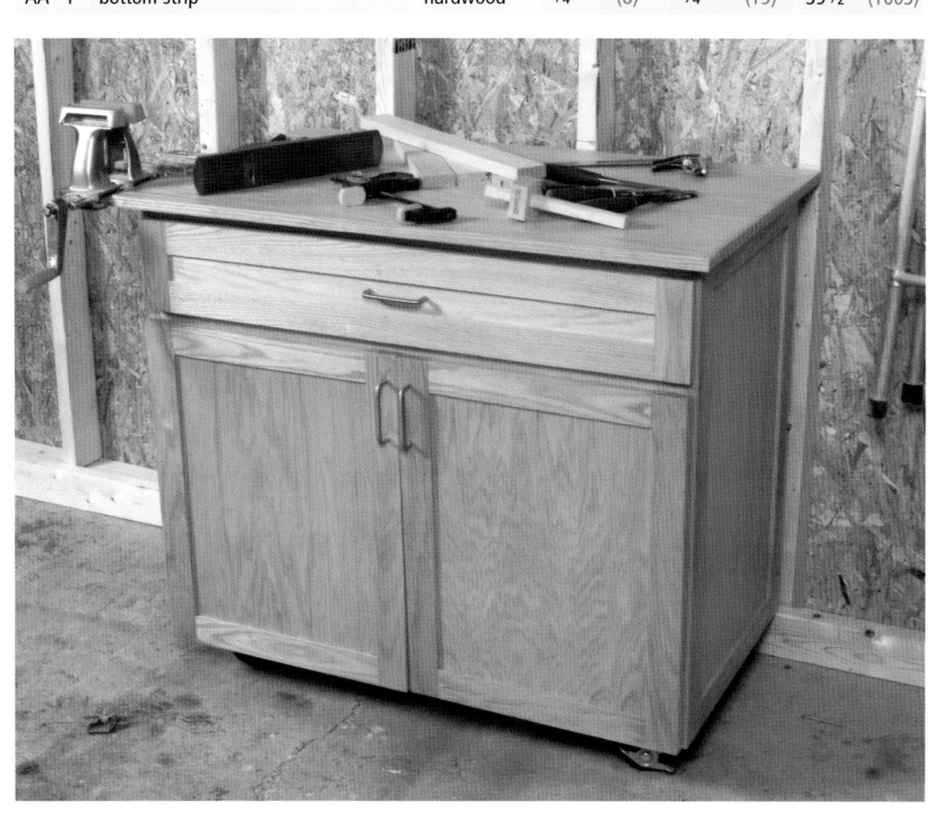

hardware & supplies

	glue
	brad nails
	colored putty
8	right-angle brackets
4	wheels
4	European-style hidden hinges and plates
3	18" (457mm) full-extension drawer glide sets
3	handles
	5/16" (8mm) lag screws
	5/16" (8mm) or 3/8" (10mm) bolts, nuts and washers
	wood plugs
	1 1/2" (38mm) screws
	1 1/4" (32mm) screws
	1" (25 mm) screws
	5/8" (16mm) screws

1 Cut the side panel stiles A and rails B to the sizes indicated in the materials list. Form a 1⁄4"-wide by 3⁄4"-deep groove (see shop tip before cutting) in the center of all stiles and rails. The side center panels C will fit into the grooves. To cut the grooves, set your table saw fence 1⁄4" away from the blade, which should be 3⁄4" above the table's top surface. Run one side edge of each board through the saw, then reverse the boards so the opposite face of each board is against the fence. Push the boards through again. This technique will center each groove on the edges of all stiles and rails. Depending on the saw blade width (kerf), you may have to run each board through the blade at the center of each groove to clean the channel.

SHOP *tip*

First, if you are ripping stiles and rails from 1x5 or 1x6 stock, keep the waste strips, as they can be used as edge strips on panels. Second, verify the thickness of the so-called 1⁄4" plywood you buy for the center panels. In many cases, it's not a true 1⁄4" thick, so your groove cut widths will have to be adjusted to fit.

2 The rails require a 3⁄4"-long by 1⁄4"-thick (or equal to the groove width) tenon on both ends. The tenons will fit into the grooves in the stiles. You can form the tenons in a number of ways, but always be sure to cut test pieces for a trial fit. Set the outside face of the blade 3⁄4" away from the saw fence. Nibble away with multiple cuts using the miter slide on each face of the rail to form the tenons. Use a tenon-cutting jig if you have one available. On each face of the rail you'll need to make a shoulder cut that's 3⁄4" from the end, before removing the waste material. Install a dado blade and fence to form the tenons. The stacked dado blade is a little expensive, but a good carbide-tipped set is a useful addition to any woodworking shop. It's normally adjustable from 1⁄8" to 13⁄16" and will be used on many of your woodworking projects. You can cut rabbets, grooves or dadoes quickly, easily and accurately with this blade.

3 Cut the center panels C for each side frame. Assemble the rails and stiles around each panel by inserting the panel and the rail tenons into the grooves. When you are sure everything fits together correctly, apply glue on the tenons and clamp until the adhesive sets. You can check the frame for square by measuring both diagonals on each assembly (see photo in step 14). Adjust if necessary by tapping lightly on the long side until both measurements are equal.

4 The back panel is 36" wide, so three back panel stiles D will be installed for added strength. Cut the stiles D and rails E to size, then form the grooves and tenons as in steps 1 and 2. One of the stiles D, which should be marked as the center stile, requires a groove on each long edge to receive the panels and rail tenons. Dry fit all the parts before starting the final assembly with the center panels.

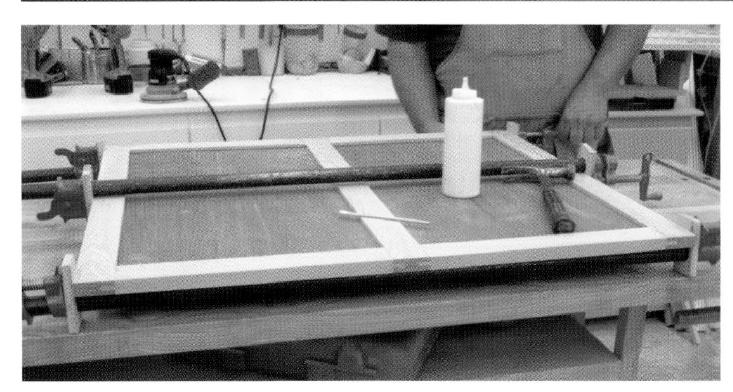

5 Prepare the two back center panels F and assemble the back frame. Use glue on the tenons and clamp the assembly until the adhesive sets.

6 Before attaching the two side panels to the back; install the bottom support cleats G and H. The cleats are set $\frac{3}{4}$" above the bottom edge of each panel and secured with glue and $1\frac{1}{4}$"-long screws. The two on the side panels are aligned flush with the side panel's front edges, leaving a $1\frac{1}{2}$" space at the back end of each panel. At this point you will have a right- and left-side panel. These cleats serve a number of purposes. They strengthen each panel, support the bottom board, provide a solid surface to attach the drawer glide hardware and properly space the pullouts to clear the door edges.

7 Join the side panels to the back panel with glue and 1½"-long screws. Counterbore the screw pilot holes so they can be filled with wood plugs and sanded smooth. Five screws in each corner will secure the panels, but space them evenly as the wood plugs will be visible. The cabinet should measure 37½" wide on the back face.

8 The bottom is a ¾"-thick piece of oak veneer plywood with a ¼"-thick strip of hardwood on the front edge. Attach the bottom strip AA to the bottom board J with glue and brad nails, then use a colored putty to fill the nail holes. Secure the bottom board to the three cleats G and H with glue and 1½"-long screws.

9 The upper and lower front rails K strengthen the cabinet, define the drawer box space and provide an upper center stop for the doors. The upper rail is installed flush with the side panels' top edges. Leave a 5" space between the two rails for the drawer box. Secure each rail end with two 1½"-long screws in counterbored holes that can be filled with ⅜"-diameter wood plugs.

10 The two upper drawers also need cleats L to support the glide hardware. The bottom edges of the top drawer's cleats are installed in line with the top edge of the lower rail. The middle drawer's cleats can be installed in any position, so allow enough space between the two bottom drawers to suit your tool storage requirements. I've aligned my cleats to have a 16" space above the bottom board. That position will let me use the lowest drawer for tall power tools like circular saws. Fasten the cleats using glue and $1\frac{1}{4}$"-long screws into the front and back stiles of the side panels.

11 Generally, drawer boxes are 1" less in height and width than the drawer opening, when using standard drawer glide hardware like the 18" full-extension glides I'm using. That rule can be used with almost all drawer glides, but check the specifications with your hardware before building the boxes. To simplify cutting, I will make all my drawer boxes the same size. Each drawer box will be 4" high and $33\frac{1}{2}$" wide. I'm using $\frac{1}{2}$"-thick Baltic birch plywood for the drawer boxes, which is a favorite material with many cabinetmakers. Each drawer side has a $\frac{1}{4}$"-deep by $\frac{1}{2}$"-wide rabbet on both ends to accept the fronts and backs N. Cut the parts to size using the same techniques that you used to cut the rail tenons.

12 The drawers are assembled using glue and brad nails. Apply glue to the rabbet cuts and attach the side boards to the front and back boards. The drawer bottom P is also attached with glue and brads.

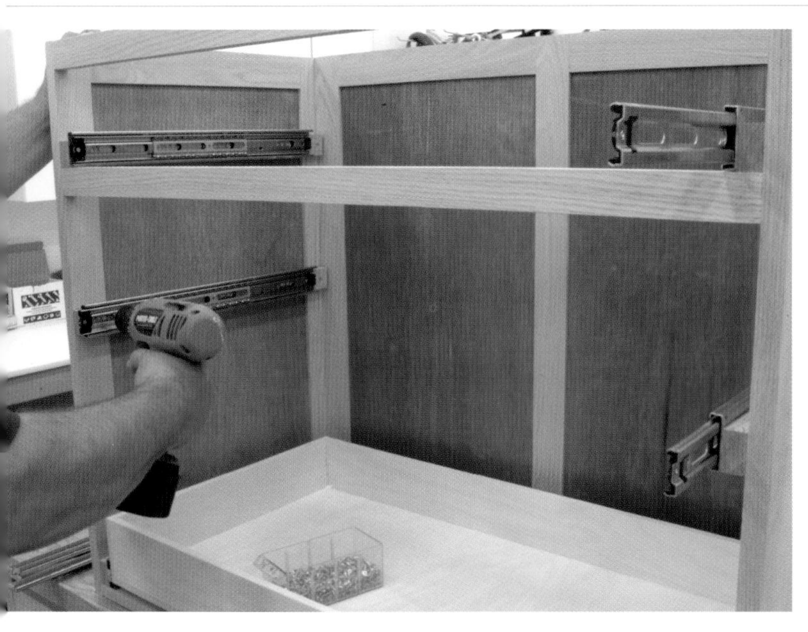

13 Install the drawer glide hardware onto the cleats G and L, following the manufacturer's instructions. Most glide hardware, as mentioned earlier, needs ½" clearance on each side of the drawer box. I'm using full-extension (FX) glides, but a standard three-quarter-extension glide will work just as well.

14 The doors are made following the same steps as the side panels. My doors are flush with the bottom edge of the cabinet and overlay the middle rail by ½". The total door height is 23½". When two doors are to be installed using European-style hidden hinges, door width is determined by adding 1" to the cabinet's interior dimension and dividing by two. The interior width of the cabinet is 36". Adding 1" and dividing by two means I'll need two 18½"-wide doors to properly fit on the cabinet. Cut all the door parts Q, R and S and construct both doors. Measure the diagonals to ensure the doors are square.

15 The drawer face is also built using frame and panel construction techniques. It's typically 1" wider than the inside cabinet width and 1" higher than the drawer space opening height. Using those guidelines, the drawer face will be 6" high and 37" wide. Using parts T, U and V, build the drawer face following the same assembly procedures as the doors.

16 The doors will be mounted using European-style hidden hinges. I'm using full-overlay 107° hinges and standard side plates. Each door needs two 35mm-diameter holes for the hinges. The holes are 4" on center from each end and drilled 1/8" away from the door edge. I recommend that you purchase a small, inexpensive drill press to make the hinge holes. This is one procedure that's difficult to do without a drill press.

17 Attach the hinges to the doors with 5/8"-long screws. Use a square to be sure the hinge arm is 90° to the door edge.

18 Connect the plates to the hinges and hold the door in its normally open position on the cabinet with a 1/8"-thick spacer between the cabinet and door. Drive 5/8"-long screws through the hinge plate holes and into the side panel stiles to anchor the hinge plates. The doors will be accurately aligned using this simple installation procedure.

19 The drawer face is attached to the box with four 1"-long screws driven through the front board and into the back of the drawer face. But first, cut the drawer-face filler W and tape it to the back of the drawer's center panel. This will prevent the drawer handle from bending the center panel. Any scrap piece of 1/4"-thick material will work fine.

20 Secure the drawer face to the box so the face is centered on the drawer opening.

21 Install single or double metal right-angle brackets to secure the top board.

22 A number of styles and materials can be used for the tool cabinet top. I discuss some of the options in the construction notes. However, for my use, a plywood veneer top will work fine. The top board X is edged with 1/4" hardwood strips Y and Z. You can cut the strips on a table saw, or purchase a suitable stock moulding at the lumber store. The strips are attached with glue and brad nails. The overall top size is 23 1/2" x 39 1/2".

23 The top is secured to the cabinet with $\frac{5}{8}$"-long screws in the right-angle brackets. I've set my top board to have a 1" overhang on each side and $1\frac{1}{2}$" overhang on the front and back face of the cabinet.

24 I've installed four heavy-duty locking wheels to my cabinet. The locking feature will be handy when I want to use the cabinet as a table saw extension or mobile workbench or for a small power tool like a grinder. Use $\frac{5}{16}$" lag screws, driven into the lower cleats, to secure the wheels. If the holes are not located under the cleats, use $\frac{5}{16}$"- or $\frac{3}{8}$"-diameter bolts, nuts and washers. Once the fit and operation of the drawers is checked and completed, apply a finish to the cabinet. I used three coats of polyurethane to finish the cabinet then installed door and drawer handles.

construction NOTES

The most important construction issue is the process of building frame and panel cabinetry, not the type of wood you use. You might want to use a lower-priced wood that can be painted or a different species that's readily available and less expensive in your area.

The purpose of this project is to practice frame and panel construction. This cabinetry style can be used to build dozens of furniture pieces for your home. Projects like entertainment centers, bedroom furniture, portable bars, cabinet doors and display cabinets can be built using frames and panels.

I used G1S (good one side) $\frac{1}{4}$" veneer plywood for my center panels because I wasn't concerned about the cabinet's interior appearance. However, the inside can be as beautiful as the outside by using G2S (good two sides) veneer plywood.

If this rolling tool cabinet will be used as a woodworking tool bench, a plywood top will be fine. But you might want to use it in the garage to work on your car or lawnmower. If that is your situation, a laminate top or possibly a metal cover for the top board would be more suitable.

Locks can be installed on the doors and drawer box. Good drawer locks are available at your local home-improvement store. One of the doors can be fastened with barrel bolts, but you'll have to set back the bottom drawer. The barrel bolts can be slid into a hole in the middle rail and in the bottom board. Then the other door can be locked to the fixed door, which should provide enough security to keep your tools tucked safely away.

However, the main focus of this project is frame and panel construction. Take your time and practice the techniques because you can use this woodworking style for hundreds of applications. And best of all, the panels can be made with any low-cost table saw, proving once again that you don't need a fortune in tools to build great furniture!

tall storage cabinets

PROJECT 5

Your workshop might be in a garage that you share with the family car, or in a basement, or you may be lucky enough to have a dedicated woodworking shop. However, all shops share a common problem — not enough storage space for those hundreds of small items and tools.

We have screws, nails, glues, cleaners, stains and finishes, dowels, biscuits and so on. It's a never-ending list of items that we need for our projects, but finding a particular item when we need it can sometimes be a real challenge. How many times have you said, "Now where did I put those handles?" These cabinets may be just the solution you need to organize your shop.

Once again, don't spend time thinking about my choice of sheet material. That's not as important as the construction procedures, which will be the same no matter what you use. I'll discuss some material and hardware options as the project is built and suggest alternatives in the construction notes at the end of the project. The important issues to consider are the cabinet's size, how many shelves you'll need, the adjustable feature of these shelves and the level of security you require. If you plan to store paints and stains in these cabinets versus hardware, you may want to install a lock on the doors.

I built two cabinets to illustrate the versatility of this design; however, you may need a different size, so look at your requirements before cutting the panels. I'll also show you how to lay out a sheet-cutting diagram, which you should do with every project to save time and materials. This is the process I go through for everything I build, and it helps me analyze my design.

I enjoy building these storage cabinets and really appreciate how they help organize a shop. These two were put to good use at my friend's auto repair shop. They help eliminate the frustration of time wasted looking for parts and supplies. I'm sure you, too, will understand how valuable these cabinets are after you begin using them in your workshop. Remember, analyze your storage requirements before beginning, because those needs determine the cabinet sizes.

Top B
Top C
Side A
Door J
Back D
Back E
Side A
Shelf F
Shelf G
Shelf F
Shelf G
1½"
1¼"
Bottom C
Side A
Bottom B
Door H
Door H
24"
16"
76"
4"

inches (millimeters)

REFERENCE	QUANTITY	PART	STOCK	THICKNESS	(mm)	WIDTH	(mm)	LENGTH	(mm)	SHEET LAYOUT IDENTIFIERS
A	4	sides	MDF	$^3/_4$	(19)	$15^1/_4$	(387)	76	(1930)	1,2,3,4
B	2	top and bottom	MDF	$^3/_4$	(19)	$15^1/_4$	(387)	$22^1/_2$	(572)	5,6
C	2	top and bottom	MDF	$^3/_4$	(19)	$15^1/_4$	(387)	$14^1/_2$	(368)	7,8
D	1	back	MDF	$^3/_4$	(19)	24	(610)	76	(1930)	9
E	1	back	MDF	$^3/_4$	(19)	16	(406)	76	(1930)	10
F	6	shelves	MDF	$^3/_4$	(19)	$15^1/_4$	(387)	$22^7/_{16}$	(570)	11,12,13,14,15,16
G	6	shelves	MDF	$^3/_4$	(19)	$15^1/_4$	(387)	$14^7/_{16}$	(367)	17,18,19,20,21,22
H	2	doors	MDF	$^3/_4$	(19)	$11^3/_4$	(298)	76	(1930)	23,24
J	1	door	MDF	$^3/_4$	(19)	$15^1/_2$	(394)	76	(1930)	25

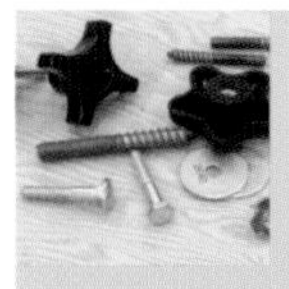

hardware & supplies

10	cabinet legs
9	107° hinges and plates
3	handles
	$1^1/_2$" (38mm) particleboard screws
	$^5/_8$" (16mm) screws
	glue
48	shelf pins

1 Before cutting the panels for any woodworking project, you should draw a sheet layout plan as shown in the illustration. Sizes are detailed, and a unique number is assigned to each part for easy identification. This step eliminates material waste and reduces errors. Review the drawing and notice the numerical identifiers on the panels. As you draw the sheets, try to group the rip sizes and crosscutting dimensions. If you plan to do a lot of projects and like the sheet layout process, you'll find a number of reasonably priced programs on the Internet. I use a software package called CutList Plus from www.cutlistplus.com.

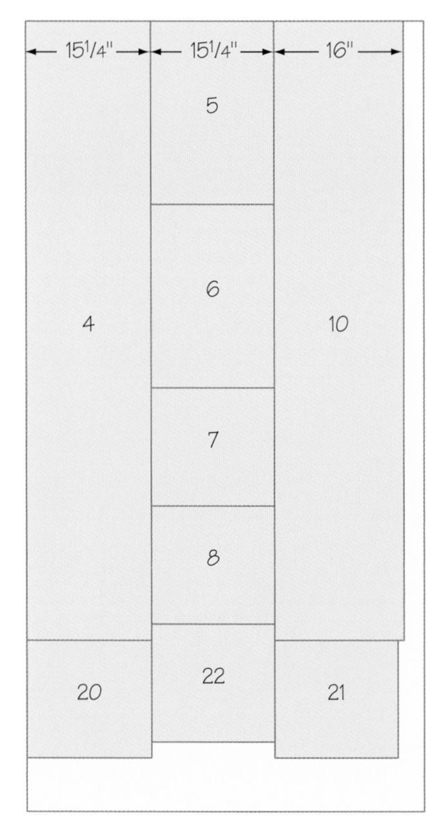

2 Cut all the panels to the sizes shown in the materials list. Review the sheet layout diagram for cutting patterns. These panels can be cut on a table saw or with a circular saw, or ripped to size by the lumberyard for a small fee. Write the panel identifier number on a nonvisible edge of each panel. Indicate the top end of each side panel so they can be positioned correctly when you drill the shelf pin holes. Numbering each panel eliminates the need to measure and hunt through a pile of cut parts trying to find the correct piece.

3 Drill one face of each side panel A with a bit to match the diameter of the shelf pins you plan to use. My holes are spaced about 1¼" apart and 1½" in from the front and back edges. Build a drilling jig, as shown in the photo, and place a wood dowel on the drill bit to limit the depth of each hole. Be sure to start the holes at the top of each side panel so they will be correctly aligned on each panel. I always try to use the numbered end of my panels as the top edge, to eliminate drilling and assembly mistakes.

SHOP *tip*

I found almost no MDF panel splitting when I used 1½"-long screws compared to the 2" screws. Keep the screws at least 1" away from the board ends and cover the edges with glue. A combination of 1½"-long particleboard screws, in drilled pilot holes with glue added, seems to be the best procedure for a strong joint.

4 Join the sides A of each case to the top and bottom boards B and C. Assemble both the 16"- and 24"-wide cases. Use glue and 1½" particleboard screws (see shop tip) for the assembly. Four screws per connection, along with yellow carpenter's glue, will form a strong joint.

5 The backs D and E are the full height and width of each cabinet. Attach them with glue and $1\frac{1}{2}$"-long screws in piloted holes that are about 8" apart.

6 Both cabinets will have plastic adjustable legs installed. Moisture and shop liquids do not affect plastic legs, so they are an ideal choice for workshop cabinets. These legs don't have a great deal of side strength, so dragging the cabinet across a floor can snap one easily. However, they have a 650-pound load rating, so they can hold just about anything you plan to store in the cabinets. The 16"-wide case has four legs, and the 24"-wide unit will have six legs. I've installed two legs in the center of the wider 24" cabinet for added support. Set the front legs 2" back from the cabinet's front edge for kick space. Position the back legs at the edge and back so the leg flange is under the side and back panel edges. The cabinet load will be transferred from the shelves to the side panels, then to the legs and finally the floor.

7 Door sizes are based on interior cabinet widths, and the rule states that the door is 1" wider than the cabinet's inside dimension. If you need two doors, then simply take that inside width dimension plus 1", and divide by 2 to find the exact width of each door. This is a frameless-style tall cabinet, so the door height equals the cabinet height. If you have access to a small router and $\frac{3}{8}$" roundover bit, ease the outside face of each door H and J to soften the look. However, each door can just as easily stay a square, flat panel.

8 Drill three 35mm-diameter hinge holes in each door for the 107° hidden hinges. Two of the holes on the doors can be located 7" from each end, and the third should be located halfway between them. Each hole is drilled $\frac{1}{8}$" away from the door edge.

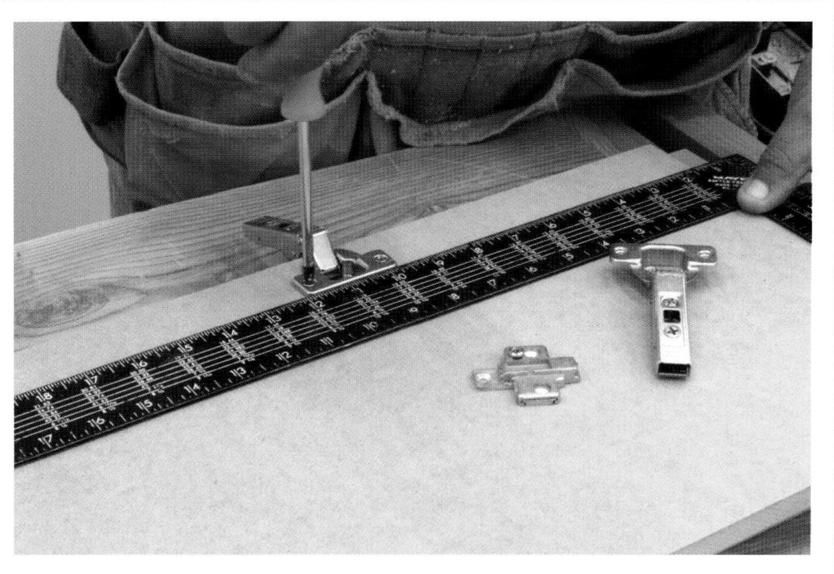

9 Attach the hinges to the door in the 35mm-diameter holes. The hinge arms should be 90° to the door's edge, so use a square to align the hinges. Use 5⁄8"-long screws to secure the hinges.

10 Doors can be accurately and easily attached to the cabinets. First, attach the hinge plates to the hinge bodies and place blocks under one corner of the cabinet to support the door so that its bottom edge is aligned with the underside of the cabinet's bottom board. Place a 1⁄8"-thick spacer between the cabinet and door while holding the door in its normally open position. The hinge plates will then be properly located. Drive 5⁄8"-long screws through the plate holes and into the cabinet side. The doors will be accurately and securely mounted once all the hinge plate screws are installed.

construction NOTES

Once all the doors are hung, install the handles. When you are satisfied that all the shelves fit and the doors work properly, remove the hardware and paint the cabinets. A good primer and one or two coats of paint will properly finish and protect your cabinets.

Someone asked why I didn't use one door on the 24"-wide cabinet. I did consider doing that, but a sheet of 3⁄4"-thick MDF weighs about 90 pounds, so a 23½"-wide door would weigh 30 to 35 pounds, and that would be quite a load for the hinges. I believe there will be less strain and longer hinge life with the two-door setup.

Use any type of sheet material you prefer to build these storage cabinets. I like MDF because it's inexpensive and won't be subjected to any moisture in my application. However, plywood, particleboard or just about any other 3⁄4"-thick sheet material can be used. It's your choice. The building procedure, not the material, is most important for this project.

If you can, purchase metal shelf pins for maximum support so you won't have to worry about overloading the shelves. These cabinets can be fitted with padlocks to keep children safe from the harmful chemicals that we sometimes use. The two-door cabinet can have a padlock installed as long as one door is secured on the inside with barrel bolts. Drill holes for the barrel in the top and bottom boards, then install the hasp on the opposite door.

If you haven't got a ready supply of plastic legs in your area, a fixed base can be used. But the legs make leveling a lot quicker, so it is worth looking for a local or mail-order supplier. They normally cost between $1 and $2 per leg.

Four sheets of MDF with hardware and legs cost less than $150 and build two great storage cabinets. That's a small price for a lot of organization in my friend's shop!

simple sawhorses

PROJECT 6

I have tools in my shop that are worth hundreds of dollars. However, I can honestly say that these $5 sawhorses have been worth more to me than any tool on many occasions. They support cabinets during construction, quickly become a temporary workbench and make a great painting platform for my mouldings. More importantly, they save my back from wear and tear because they support my work at a comfortable level.

As you can see, these sawhorses are made with construction-grade lumber. If you want something a bit fancier, use a better grade of wood, but the cost rises dramatically. The only hardware involved is two carriage bolts, washers and wing nuts. This hardware can be used again when the time comes to build new sawhorses. Once the hardware is paid for, all you have to buy is a couple of 8' 2×4s.

One of the major advantages of this sawhorse design is the storage size. The feet can be quickly removed and attached flat to the legs. You can hang them on hooks in your garage or put them in the trunk of your car for transport to a job site. I usually have three or four sawhorses in my truck when I'm working at a client's house, because I know they'll be needed.

My sawhorses are beaten and bruised, covered in paint and stain, left in the rain and generally abused over the course of a year. So every once in a while I spend a couple of hours and build six or eight new units. I wouldn't be without these great helpers, and you won't either, once you build and use them in your workshop.

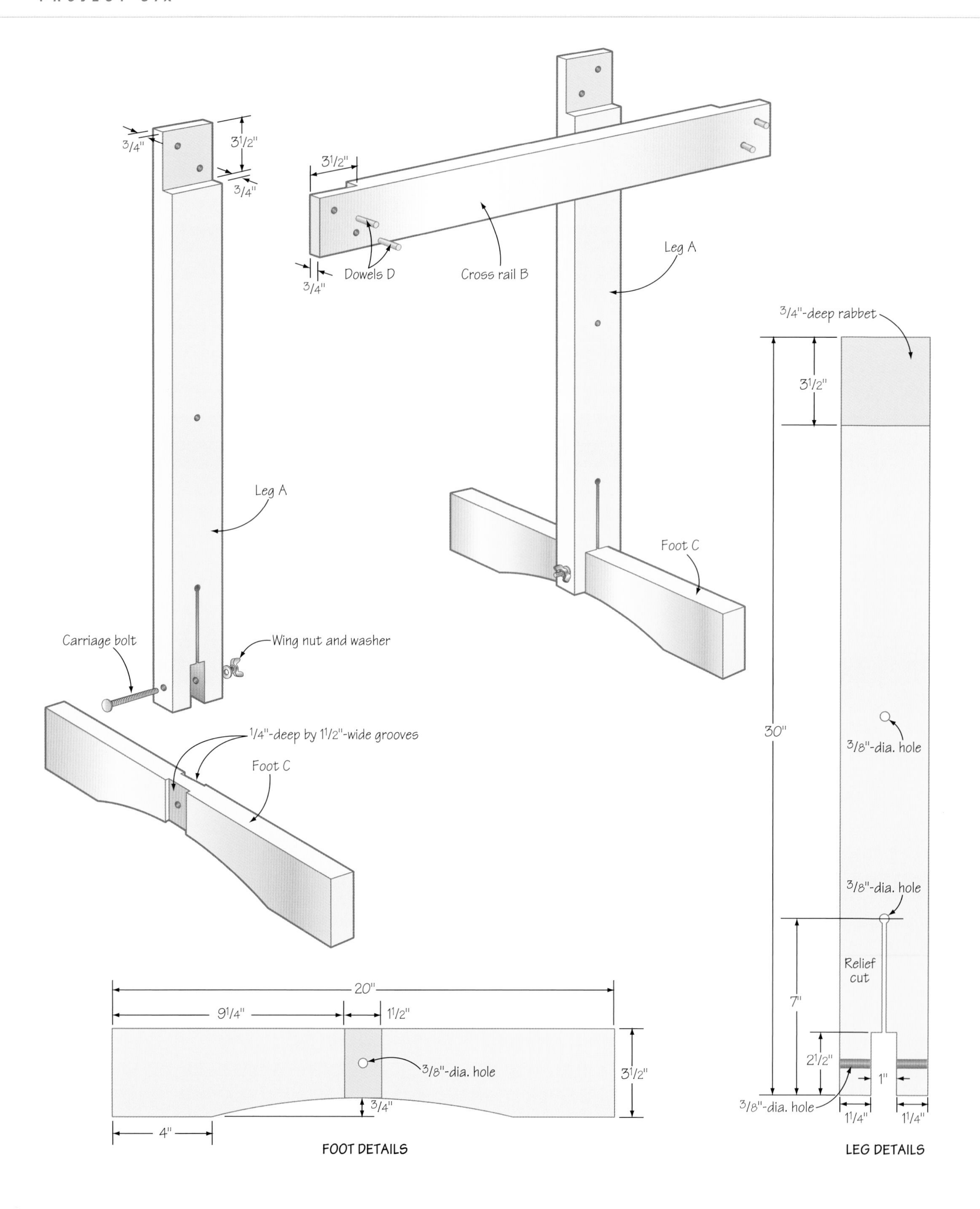
3/4"
3 1/2"
3/4"
3 1/2"
Dowels D
3/4"
Cross rail B
Leg A
Leg A
Carriage bolt
Wing nut and washer
Foot C
1/4"-deep by 1 1/2"-wide grooves
Foot C
3/4"-deep rabbet
3 1/2"
30"
3/8"-dia. hole
3/8"-dia. hole
Relief cut
7"
2 1/2"
1"
3/8"-dia. hole
1 1/4"
1 1/4"
20"
9 1/4"
1 1/2"
3/8"-dia. hole
3 1/2"
3/4"
4"
FOOT DETAILS
LEG DETAILS

inches (millimeters)

REFERENCE	QUANTITY	PART	STOCK	THICKNESS	(mm)	WIDTH	(mm)	LENGTH	(mm)
A	2	legs	pine	$1^1/_2$	(38)	$3^1/_2$	(89)	30	(762)
B	1	cross rail	pine	$1^1/_2$	(38)	$3^1/_2$	(89)	30	(762)
C	2	feet	pine	$1^1/_2$	(38)	$3^1/_2$	(89)	30	(762)
D	4	dowels	hardwood	$^5/_{16}$ dia.	(8)			2	(51)

hardware & supplies

2	$^5/_{16}$" x 4" (8mm x 102mm) carriage bolts
2	$^5/_{16}$" (8mm) washers
2	$^5/_{16}$" (8mm) wing nuts
	glue

1 Cut the two legs A and the cross rail B to the sizes shown in the materials list. Set the rail on top of the legs, flush with the top edge, and draw reference lines to indicate the rabbet cut sizes and placement. You'll need one line on each leg and two on the cross rail.

2 The legs need a $^3/_4$"-deep by $3^1/_2$"-long rabbet cut on the top end. The rail requires the same cut on each end. When joined, two rabbet cuts will form a half-lap joint. Set the outside face of your saw blade $3^1/_2$" away from your saw fence. Use the miter slide in continuous passes to nibble away at the wood. If you have a dado blade for your saw, the process will be much quicker. You can also make the cuts with a band saw if you have one.

3 Apply glue to the rabbets, then clamp the leg and rail at the half-lap joints. Place scrap lumber under the joints as you will be installing dowels in drilled holes through each joint.

4 Drill two $\frac{5}{16}$"-diameter holes through each joint. Use 2"-long by $\frac{5}{16}$"-diameter dowels with glue applied and drive them through the joints. These dowels will be sanded flush once the glue dries.

SHOP *tip*

I use and build a lot of these simple sawhorses. To avoid drawing the arc each time, I've created a template jig to quickly mark the cut line.

5 Cut the feet C to size and form a 1½"-wide by ¼"-deep dado on opposite faces, which will form a 1"-thick bridge on each foot. The dadoes are located in the center of the feet. The dadoes can be cut on a table saw with a standard or dado blade.

6 The feet require an arc, which starts 4" from each end and is ¾" high in the center, to lessen contact points with the floor for better stability. Use a template, then cut the arc with a jigsaw or scroll saw.

7 Drill a 3⁄8"-diameter hole, centered on each leg, 7" up from the bottom edge. This hole prevents splitting of the legs once the relief cut is completed, which will draw the two halves tight. Use a jigsaw to make the relief cuts. Run the saw along a line that's centered on the leg, to the hole center.

8 Cut a 1"-wide notch at the bottom of each leg. This notch should be centered on the leg and is 2½" long. Use a jigsaw to cut out the notch. The notch will allow the legs to fit in the foot dadoes. As shown, I've created a notch pattern jig for accurate and repetitive cuts.

9 This step is optional. If you have a router and 3⁄8"-radius roundover bit, ease all face corners. The roundover doesn't add anything to the sawhorses structurally, but the construction-grade lumber looks a little nicer.

10 Put the leg assembly on the feet and drill a ⅜"-diameter hole 1¼" up from each leg bottom. The hole will be drilled through both leg and foot. Thread a 4"-long carriage bolt through the hole and secure the assembly with a washer and wing nut. The bolt and nut will secure the foot to the leg, but can be easily removed for storage.

11 The final step is to drill a ⅜"-diameter hole at the halfway point on each leg to attach the feet for storage.

construction NOTES

As I mentioned, these sawhorses are worth a great deal more to me than the $5 cost to build them. However, if you want a better-looking unit, you can use any type of hardwood.

The height and width of these units are dimensions I decided would work best for my needs. You can change the width or height to suit your work by varying the legs and cross rail lengths. If you want a sawhorse that's almost impossible to tip over, lengthen the feet. They are, however, very steady with 20" feet.

The same design can be used to build extra-sturdy horses using 4x4 (3½" square) lumber. Lateral support rails can be attached to both sides of two sawhorses with a plywood top installed if you need a strong workbench that can be easily assembled on a job site. Or, four sawhorses supporting a 30"-wide by 96"-long sheet of ¾" plywood also make a great workbench.

Use wood dowels and glue to join the legs to the cross rails. If you'd rather not use dowels, two 1¼"-long screws, driven through each joint, will work just as well as long as the joint is glued.

Finally, an outdoor version of this sawhorse can be built using a weather-resistant wood and polyurethane adhesive. To further protect the horses outside, apply a couple of coats of paint.

rolling shop cart

PROJECT 7

The rolling shop cart is another must-have in my shop. I use it every day to move cut panels and lumber around the shop. It, and versions like it, continue to be just as valuable as my workbench.

My carts are normally made with low-cost construction-grade lumber. The top, middle and bottom shelves are inexpensive particleboard or plywood sheeting. They are often made with cutoffs and leftover panels that are on my wood rack. In fact, the only costly items are the metal wheel casters that I use to move the carts around the shop.

These carts are not restricted to a woodshop. I use mine when I have to work on my trailer or truck, because they are perfect tool trays. In the garage, these carts can be used as mobile workbenches for repairs around the home or as handy worktables for garden potting and planting. However, be warned, as soon as the gardener in your home spots this great three-shelf cart, you'll have to make another one for yourself.

I enjoy my power tools, but this rolling cart is more valuable than any tool I have when I have to move a dozen pieces of wood around the shop. I'm sure you'll appreciate its value after building one for your shop.

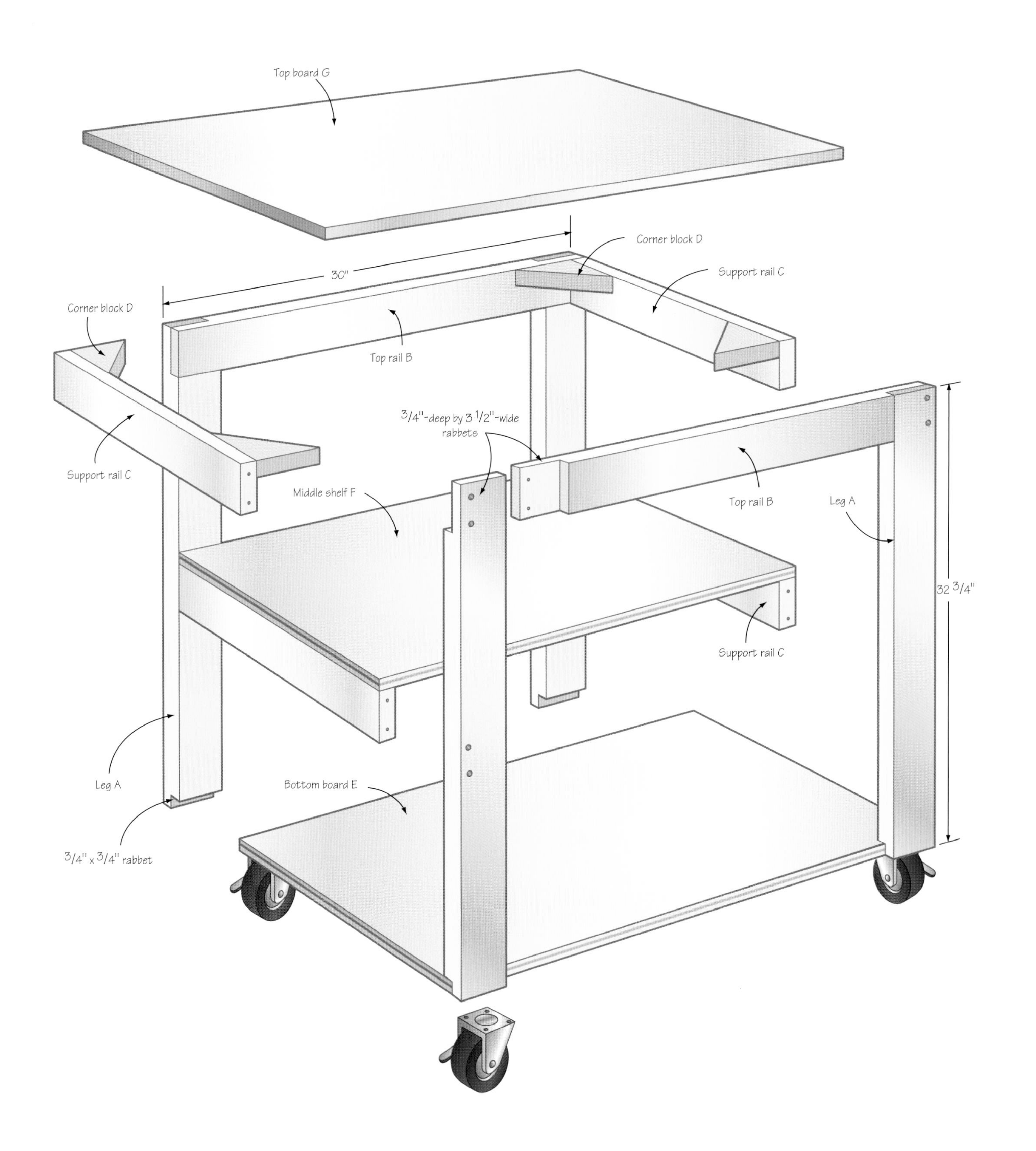
Top board G
30"
Corner block D
Support rail C
Corner block D
Top rail B
3/4"-deep by 3 1/2"-wide rabbets
Support rail C
Middle shelf F
Top rail B
Leg A
32 3/4"
Support rail C
Leg A
Bottom board E
3/4" x 3/4" rabbet

inches (millimeters)

REFERENCE	QUANTITY	PART	STOCK	THICKNESS	(mm)	WIDTH	(mm)	LENGTH	(mm)	COMMENTS
A	4	legs	pine	1½	(38)	3½	(89)	32¾	(832)	
B	2	top rails	pine	1½	(38)	3½	(89)	30	(762)	
C	4	support rails	pine	1½	(38)	3½	(89)	21	(533)	
D	4	corner blocks	pine	3½	(89)	3½	(89)			angle cut at 45°
E	1	bottom board	particleboard	¾	(19)	22½	(572)	30	(762)	
F	1	middle shelf	particleboard	¾	(19)	21	(533)	30	(762)	
G	1	top board	particleboard	¾	(19)	26	(660)	32	(813)	

hardware & supplies

	¾" (19mm) screws
	1¼" (32mm) screws
	1½" (38mm) screws
	2" (51mm) screws
	3" (76mm) screws
	nails
	glue
4	wheel assemblies

1 I want the finished height of my cart to be 36", which is the same height as my workbench. The top is ¾" thick, and I'm using wheels that are 2½" high. The side frames should then be 32¾" high, and I'll build them 30" wide. Each of the four legs A requires a ¾"-wide by ¾"-deep rabbet on one end. These rabbets can be cut on a table saw using a standard blade by nibbling out the waste materials with multiple passes. If you have a dado blade, the rabbets can be cut very quickly.

2 Each top rail B needs a rabbet that's ¾" deep by 3½" wide on both ends. The legs A also need the same-size rabbet on the uncut ends. The larger top rabbet is cut on the same face as the rabbet on the opposite end. The larger rabbet cuts on the top rails and legs will form a half-lap joint.

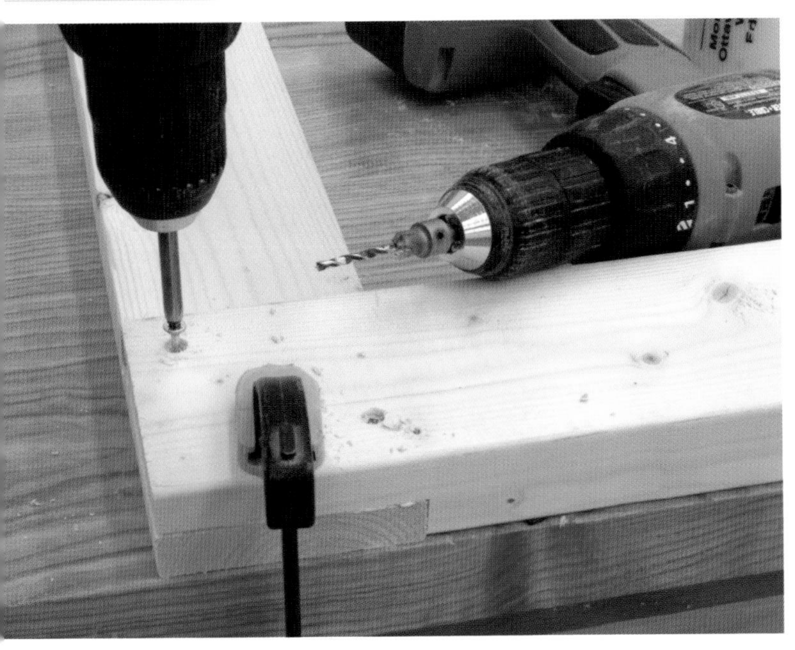

3 The half-lap joint is secured with glue and $1^1/_4$"-long screws. Or you can use glue and wood dowels as detailed in project six for the sawhorses. Build the two frames using two legs and one top rail for each assembly. Be sure to apply wood glue to all surfaces of the rabbet cuts before clamping and securing with screws.

4 The frames can now be connected to each other using the support rails C. Two are at the top, flush with the top surface of the legs, and two are attached with their top edges 16" above the lower leg ends. Attach the rails to both frames with a simple butt joint and glue. Use two 3"-long screws, in pilot holes, to secure each joint. Corner blocks will strengthen these connections. Position the leg frames so the lower rabbet cuts on the legs face inward (or face each other).

5 Glue and nail the four corner blocks D in the top corners. They should be set flush with the top edge of the cart frame.

6 The bottom board E is a piece of $^3/_4$"-thick particleboard. Cut it to the size given in the materials list and install it in the $^3/_4$" rabbets at the bottom of each leg. Use glue and two 2"-long screws at each corner to secure this panel.

7 While the cart is upside down, attach the four wheel assemblies. I used a combination of 3⁄4"- and 1½"-long screws to secure the wheels. The longer screws are positioned over the leg ends and are driven through the bottom board into the legs.

8 The middle shelf F is attached using four 2"-long screws. I don't want to use glue for this shelf, in case it has to be replaced in the future.

9 The top board G is 2" wider and longer than the cart frame. That dimension will provide a 1" overhang on all edges. Attach the top with 2"-long screws through the corner blocks. Use a sander to round over the top board's corners to prevent injury.

construction NOTES

This rolling cart is made using construction-grade framing lumber. If you want something a little better looking, use hardwood for the legs and rails. Be sure to counterbore the screw holes and fill them with wood plugs. You can always use mortise-and-tenon joints for the corner connections in place of the half-lap joints if you wish.

The finished height and width of your rolling cart should be tailored to your needs. My workbench is 36" high, but yours may not be, so change the cart height to match your bench. The cart width is fine for my shop, but you might want something different, so cut the support rails C shorter or longer to suit your needs.

My cart shelves are made of particleboard, however, plywood is stronger and can also be used. The wheels can be exchanged for heavy–duty models, along with plywood shelves to accommodate heavy loads. My shop floor is reasonably smooth concrete, but if it was rough I'd switch to a larger-diameter wheel.

My carts get bumped, bruised and beaten, which is why I use low-cost construction-grade lumber and particleboard shelves. The materials are inexpensive, so the carts can be rebuilt without spending a lot of money. However, even with the low-cost materials, these rolling carts are usable for five or six years in my shop.

hand tool wall cabinet

PROJECT 8

I believe every shop should have a dedicated wall cabinet for hand tools. Your woodworking shop might be in a garage or the basement of your home, or you may be lucky enough to have a separate shop built on your property. The physical layout doesn't matter, because we all have planes, chisels, turning tools or carving knives that should be protected from dust and dirt.

Many of us store these tools on open shelving, so they are usually scattered all over the shop. When they require cleaning and sharpening we have to hunt and gather these tools, along with our sharpening equipment, which is a waste of valuable shop time. Why not keep all these tools in one cabinet with doors, which will extend their useful service as well as reduce the time required to maintain them? This project will address those needs and, as an added bonus, show you how to build cabinet doors with acrylic center panels so everyone can see these wonderful tools.

I do not like using glass for door panels in a workshop. A flying piece of wood from a machine, or a long board being carried into the shop can easily break the glass and cause a serious accident. Acrylics, sometimes referred to by trade names such as Plexiglas, are the answer because they won't shatter when hit.

This project will show you more about dado blade usage on a table saw. And if you plan to buy one accessory in the near future, a carbide-tipped stacked dado blade set is one of the best investments you can make. It will double the usefulness of your saw because you'll be able to quickly and accurately cut dadoes, grooves and rabbet joints as well as tenons and finger joints. I'll also show you how to make another valuable accessory for your saw that will let you crosscut long boards with increased safety. This crosscutting panel jig can be made for less than $10, but you'll soon discover its true value.

This cabinet will be used to store hand tools and water baths with stones. However, it isn't limited to that particular use. A wood carver could use it for small carving tools; a scroll saw enthusiast may want to store small patterns and jigs; or you might simply need a dedicated storage area for drill, shaper and router bits. When you need safe, easily accessible, relatively dust-free storage with easy-to-see-through doors, this is the cabinet for your shop.

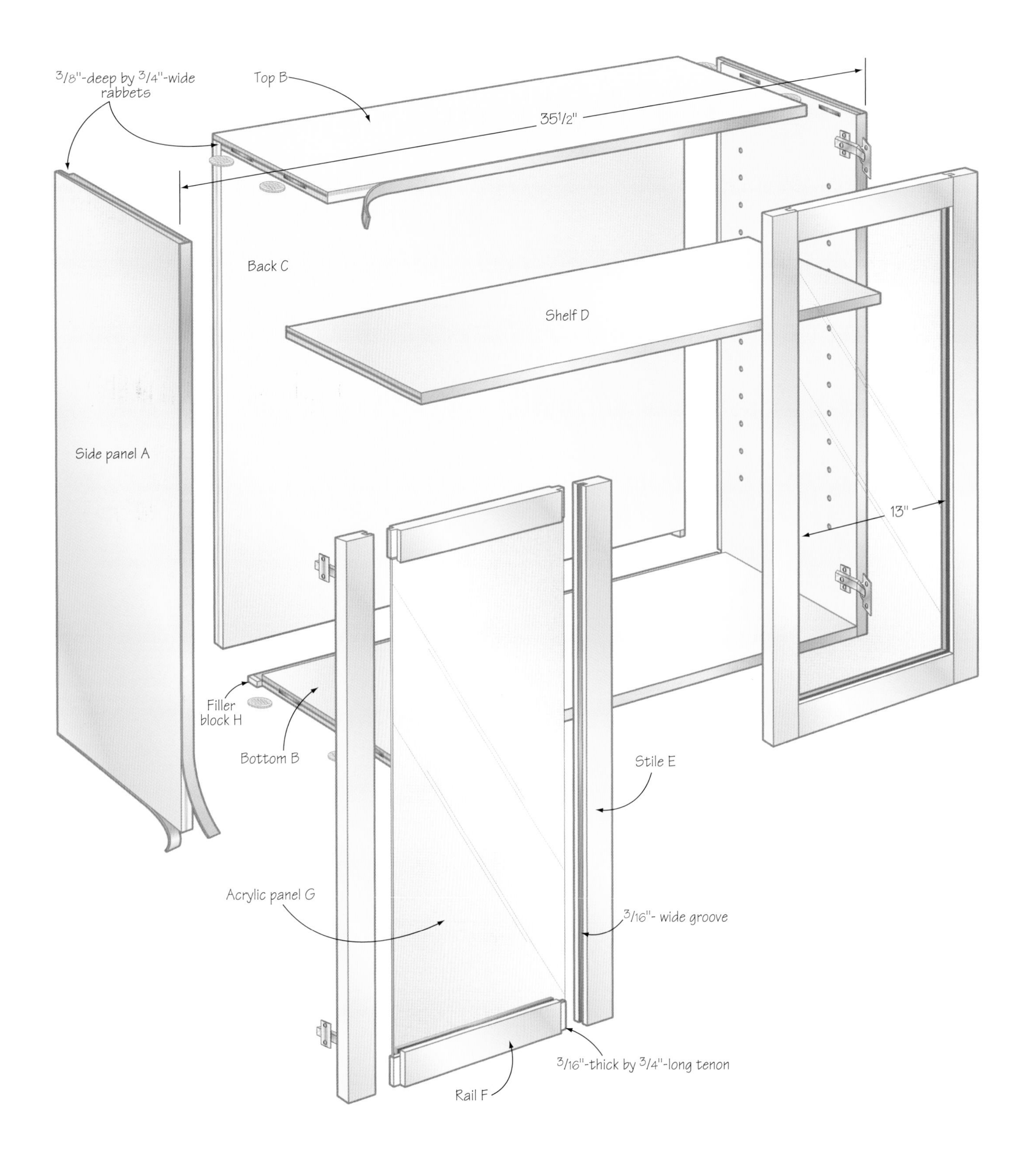
3/8"-deep by 3/4"-wide rabbets
Top B
35 1/2"
Back C
Shelf D
Side panel A
13"
Filler block H
Bottom B
Stile E
Acrylic panel G
3/16"- wide groove
3/16"-thick by 3/4"-long tenon
Rail F

inches (millimeters)

REFERENCE	QUANTITY	PART	STOCK	THICKNESS	(mm)	WIDTH	(mm)	LENGTH	(mm)
A	2	side panels	veneer ply	3/4	(19)	12	(305)	27	(686)
B	2	top and bottom	veneer ply	3/4	(19)	12	(305)	34	(864)
C	1	back	veneer ply	3/4	(19)	26 1/4	(667)	34 3/4	(883)
D	2	shelves	veneer ply	3/4	(19)	11 1/4	(286)	33 15/16	(862)
E	4	stiles	hardwood	3/4	(19)	2 1/4	(57)	27	(686)
F	4	rails	hardwood	3/4	(19)	2 1/4	(57)	14 1/2	(368)
G	2	panels	acrylic	1/8	(3)	14 1/2	(368)	24	(610)
H		filler block							

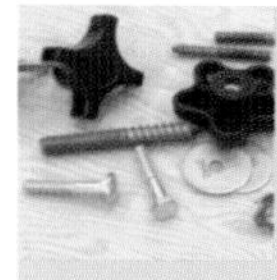

hardware & supplies

	glue
	finishing nails
	No. 20 biscuits
4	European-style hidden hinges and plates
	wood-veneer edge tape
8	handles
8	5/8" (16mm) screws
	shelf pins

SHOP *tip*

Some wood edge tapes are difficult to trim with a knife because the cut tends to follow the grain pattern. If you have a router and flush-trim bit with a bearing guide, use that method. If not, use a very sharp knife and trim the edges smooth.

1 Before you begin, refer to the end of this chapter and read the sidebar called "Making a Crosscutting Panel Jig." You can build this inexpensive jig for your table saw to safely crosscut the long ripped panels for the cabinet case.

2 Cut the side panels A and top and bottom B for the wall cabinet cases. Apply wood-veneer edge tape (to match the sheet material you are using) to the front (one long edge) of each panel. I'm using a preglued iron-on wood-veneer tape.

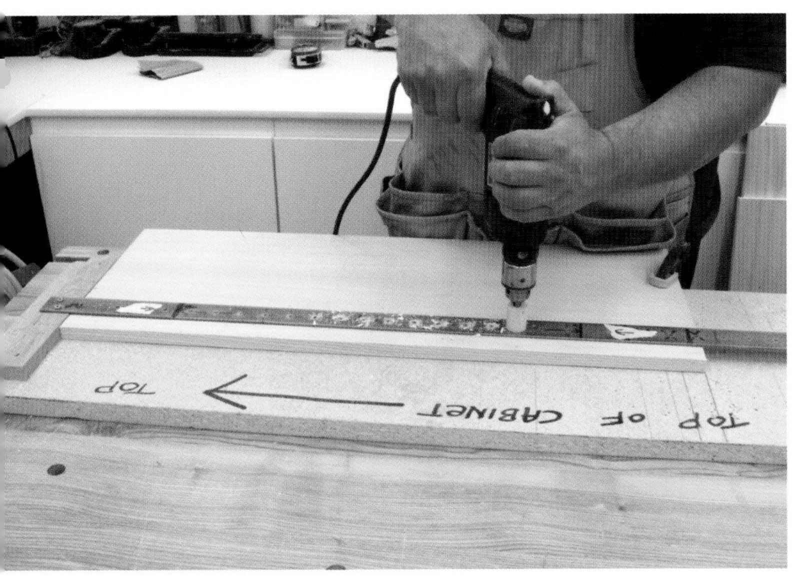

3 Drill two columns of holes in each side panel A. The hole diameter should match your choice of shelf pins. The hole columns are about 2" in from each long edge and spaced about 1½" apart. Remember to start the holes from the top edge of each side panel and on each inside face so the wood-veneer taped edges are facing in the same direction. You can easily drill the holes using the jig shown. The jig is simply a flat piece of metal with evenly spaced drilled holes and stop supports at each end. I have a wood dowel rod on the bit to limit the hole depth.

5 The two side panels A can be rabbeted on both ends and joined to the top and bottom B with glue, then clamped until the adhesive sets. Or you can use glue and finishing nails to secure the bottom and top boards in the side panel end rabbets if you don't have long clamps. However, I'm using butt joinery and biscuits to assemble my case. If you have a biscuit joiner, you might want to consider this method for your cabinet. Cut biscuit slots at the 3" and 9" marks, measured from each front edge, on each panel. Put glue on the edges and in the biscuit slots, insert No. 20 biscuits and clamp the case until the adhesive sets. If you want to learn more about biscuit joinery, pick up a copy of *The Biscuit Joiner Project Book* by Jim Stack, published by Popular Woodworking Books.

4 Before you start to assemble the case, cut a ⅜"-deep by ¾"-wide rabbet on the inside back face of each side panel A and top and bottom B. A router or dado blade on your table saw will easily cut the plywood veneer panels.

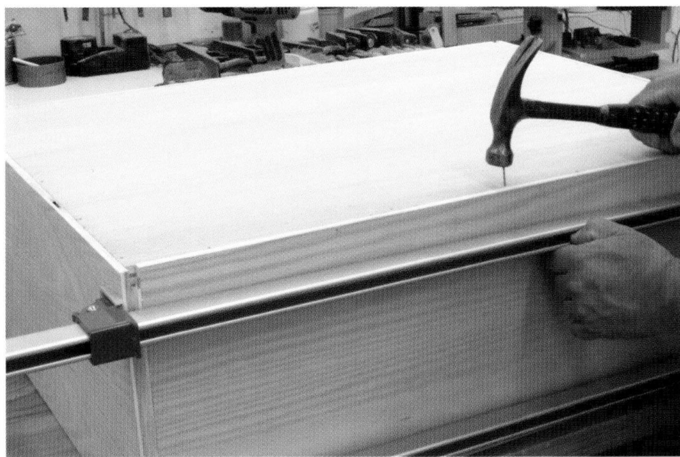

6 Cut the back C, apply glue to the rabbet cuts and set the panel in place. Use finishing nails to secure the panel so the glue will properly set up.

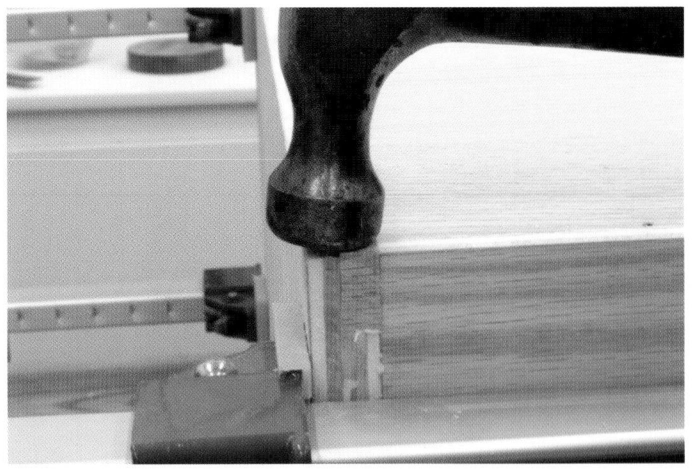

7 Fill the rabbet cuts on the bottom of the cabinet with small filler blocks H. Use glue to secure these fillers and sand flush when the adhesive sets. They will provide a flat surface for the wood-veneer edge tape that will be applied to cover the lower end cuts of the side boards.

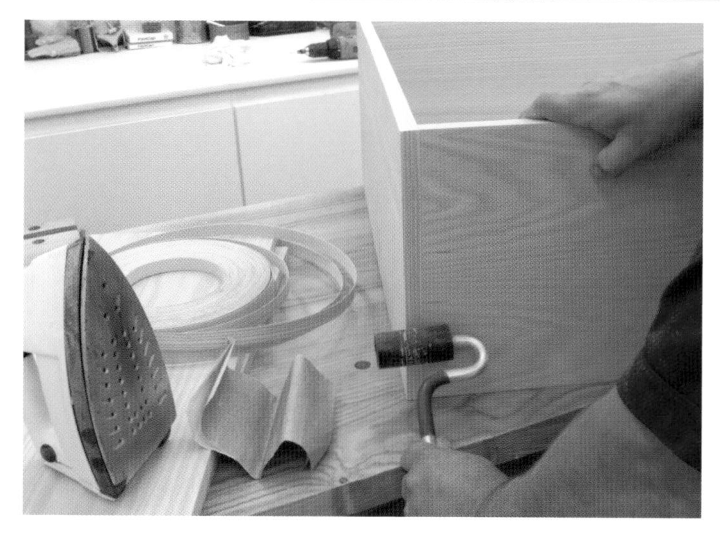

8 Cut the two shelves D to the size noted in the materials list. Apply wood-veneer edge tape to the front edge of each shelf. While your iron is hot, put edge tape on the bottom (visible) ends of each side panel A. The top ends of the side panels won't be seen, so they don't need to be covered.

9 The doors are at the full cabinet height of 27", which is typical with frameless-style upper cabinets. The door width, using European-style hidden hinges, is 1" greater than the inside cabinet dimension of 34". If you require two doors, which is the case with this cabinet, divide the inside dimension of 34" plus 1", by two. Therefore, the cabinet will need two doors 17½" wide by 27" high. All stiles (vertical members) and rails (horizontal members) are 2¼" wide. Prepare all the door parts (stiles E and rails F), remembering that the 14½" length of each rail includes material to cut ¾"-long tenons on each end. Each of the eight door members requires a ¾"-deep by $^{3}/_{16}$"-wide groove on one long edge. The groove will hold the rail tenons and the ⅛"-thick acrylic center panel G.

10 The tenon on both ends of the four rails is $^{3}/_{16}$" thick by ¾" long. It can be cut by making multiple passes over a standard table saw blade or in one pass using a stacked dado blade set on your table saw.

11 The door frames can now be partially assembled for other machine work and finishing at this point. Glue and clamp one rail to the stiles. Dry fit the other rail because it will be removed later to install the acrylic center panel. Use a ⅜" roundover bit in your router to soften the outside perimeter of each door frame. Once the machine work is complete, apply a finish to the cabinet and door frames.

12 Once your finish has dried, remove the nonglued rail and install the acrylic panel G in each door. Apply glue to the rail tenons and clamp the frames until the adhesive cures.

SHOP *tip*

The grooves on all the rails and stiles are 3⁄16" wide, and the acrylic panels I'm using are 1⁄8" thick. The added 1⁄16" of groove width will allow the panels to float so the stiles and rails can expand and contract with seasonal changes.

13 Install two 100° to 120° hinges on each door, in 35mm-diameter hinge holes. Drill the hinge holes about 4" from each door end and 1⁄8" away from the door edge. Use 5⁄8" screws to secure the hinges, making sure they are at right angles to the door edge.

14 Clip the hinge plate on the hinges and install the doors on the cabinet. Hold the door in its normally open position on the cabinet, with a 1⁄8" spacer between the door and cabinet side panel edge. Drive 5⁄8" screws through the hinge plate holes into the cabinet side. The doors will be properly mounted and aligned using this simple technique. Install the door handles to complete the cabinet.

Making a Crosscutting Panel Jig

STEP 1 Cut a piece of 3⁄4"-thick sheet material that's approximately 24" wide by 36" long. You'll also need a strip of hardwood that fits snugly, without binding, in one of the miter slots on your table saw. The hardwood strip should be about 30" long, so a few inches of the material will extend past the front and rear edges of the sheet material. Most miter slots are 3⁄4" wide and about 1⁄4" to 3⁄8" deep. Attach the hardwood strip to the bottom face of the panel, parallel to one 24"-long edge. Draw a line parallel to the panel's edge to guide the strip placement, being sure to mark it so that 1" of panel extends past the blade.

STEP 2 Place the panel, with the hardwood strip attached, in the miter slot and cut the panel overhang. This cut will align the panel travel parallel to the saw blade.

STEP 3 Use a carpenter's framing square to align a 1½"-wide by 3⁄4"-thick hardwood guide at 90° to the panel's cut edge. Panels are to be cut crest against the hardwood guide and pushed through the saw blade on the panel jig. Secure the guide with screws.

construction NOTES

I've used acrylic for my center panels, but you can use plywood veneer or glass. However, for safety reasons I would not use glass panel doors in a workshop, and I strongly suggest you don't, either. The acrylic sheets are inexpensive and will not shatter if something strikes them. If you do decide to use glass, make sure it is tempered, so it will not shatter if broken.

My cabinet is about 35½" wide by 27" high, because that size meets my requirements. However, the cabinet can be any size using the same construction steps. I've used wood shelves, but 1⁄4"-thick acrylic can also be used for the shelving if you want to install a light in the cabinet to illuminate the interior. The cabinet depth is also variable should you want to store bigger equipment. The size doesn't matter — it's the building steps that are important.

How would you join your cabinet box? As earlier suggested, you might want to cut side panel end rabbets and use glue, or you might want to use screws and glue. Also, the cabinet back can be overlapped instead of inset in the rabbets. A 1⁄4"-thick sheet of veneer plywood might also be an option for your back panel.

I've used oak veneer plywood to build my cabinet and sprayed three coats of lacquer on all wood surfaces. However, your can use almost any sheet material, such as melamine particleboard or plywood, and paint the cabinet. If cost is an issue, use 3⁄4" particleboard or MDF for the cabinet carcass and doors, then apply a couple coats of oil-based paint to all surfaces.

The doors can be made of sheet material if you don't need to see the cabinet interior. Install a latch on one door and padlock hasp on the front if you need a secure cabinet for expensive tools, or one that you don't want accessible to children. You can build a few of these cabinets using melamine particleboard, as I have in my shop, with solid, flat panel melamine doors for tool and hardware storage. Most of the cabinets in my shop are white melamine to reflect as much light as possible and maximize my storage.

And finally, don't limit this cabinet construction method as shop storage only. This design can be used anywhere in your home. How about upper cabinets over the washer and dryer, wall cabinets in the children's room for toys and books, added storage for your home office or possibly a few nice wall cabinets with glass panels for the kitchen?

base cabinet work center

PROJECT 9

We often think of a woodworking work center as the traditional wood bench. In many cases, that's the common and typical setup — a heavy wood top supported by thick wood legs. However, many woodworkers need a different style of bench. Carvers, scroll saw enthusiasts, small crafts builders and pattern makers need a center that has a smooth top and a comfortable place to sit. Plenty of storage for their tools and supplies is more valuable to them than a large wood bench.

This work center details the construction of base cabinets built in the frameless style. It has one three-drawer cabinet and one with two pullout trays behind a door. The cabinets support a medium-density fiberboard (MDF) top. However, there are a number of other options for the top, and I'll discuss a few for your consideration in the construction notes at the end of the project.

This frameless case construction method is the same no matter which configuration of doors, drawers or pullouts you decide to install. I haven't shown a simple base with adjustable shelves, because it uses the same case with the added step of drilling columns of adjustable shelf pin holes before the case is assembled.

My work center top is 5' long, and is supported on each end by an 18"-wide base cabinet. That will leave a 24" open space that can be used to store a stool or trash container. The space also provides leg room so a shop stool can be pulled close to the table surface when someone is seated. That's an important feature if you are carving or scroll sawing and want to get close to your work at a lower level. We think most woodworking is done while standing at our workbench or power tools, but a large percentage of woodworkers like or need to work seated.

Woodworkers who use table saws and lathes will also appreciate this work center. It's great for reading or drawing plans, and the storage features are always a welcome addition in any shop. Do you need to sit and sharpen a few tools, study a plan, make a couple of phone calls and take notes, or just sit and relax with a cup of coffee for a few minutes in your shop? If you do, this is the project for you.

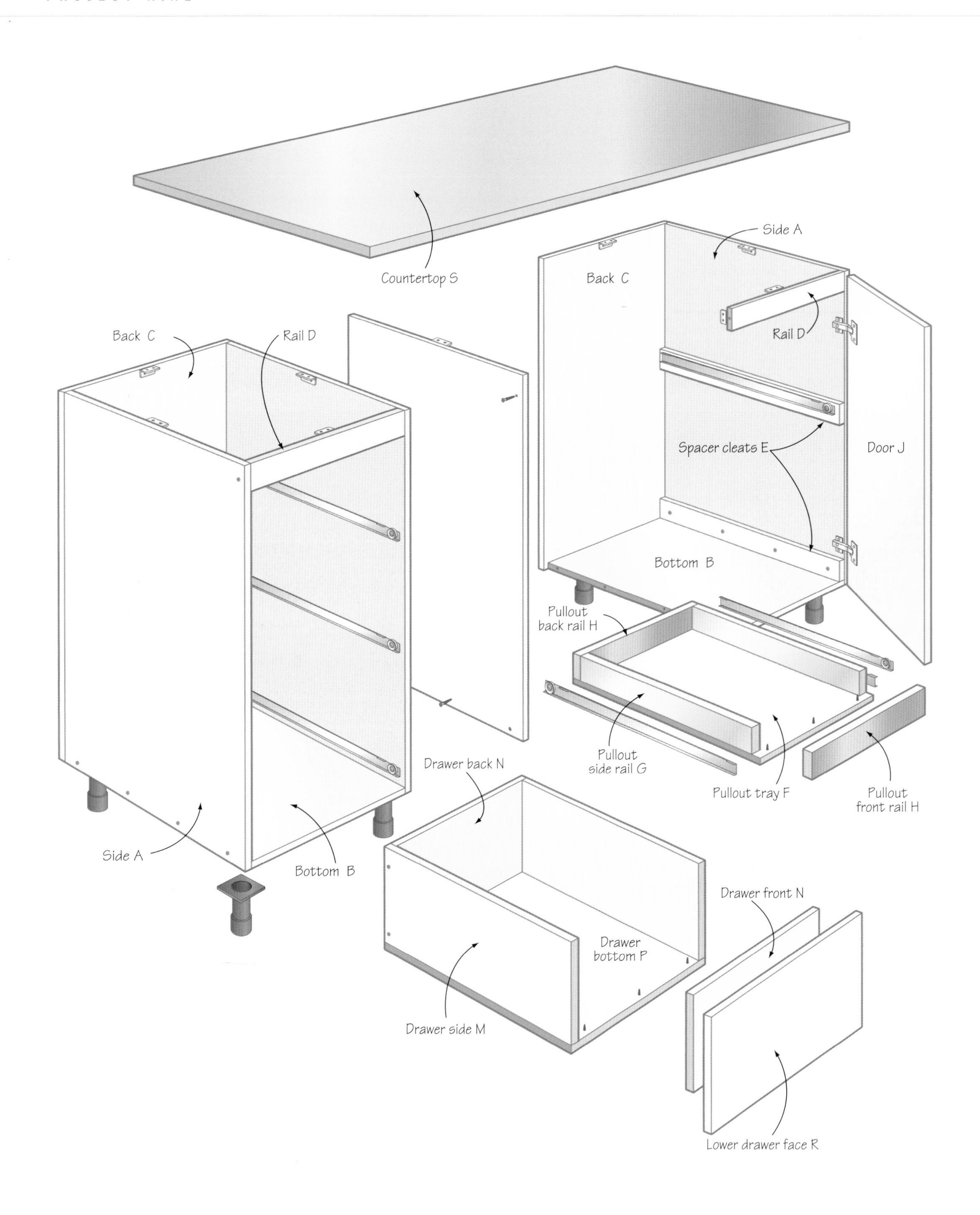
Countertop S
Side A
Back C
Rail D
Back C
Rail D
Spacer cleats E
Door J
Bottom B
Pullout back rail H
Pullout side rail G
Pullout tray F
Pullout front rail H
Drawer back N
Side A
Bottom B
Drawer front N
Drawer bottom P
Drawer side M
Lower drawer face R

inches (millimeters)

REFERENCE	QUANTITY	PART	STOCK	THICKNESS	(mm)	WIDTH	(mm)	LENGTH	(mm)
CABINETS									
A	4	sides	melamine PB	5/8	(16)	23 3/8	(594)	31	(787)
B	2	bottoms	melamine PB	5/8	(16)	23 3/8	(594)	16 3/4	(425)
C	2	backs	melamine PB	5/8	(16)	18	(457)	31	(787)
D	2	rails	melamine PB	5/8	(16)	2	(51)	16 3/4	(425)
E	2	spacer cleats	melamine PB	5/8	(16)	2	(51)	23 3/8	(594)
PULLOUTS									
F	2	pullout trays	melamine PB	5/8	(16)	15 1/8	(384)	22	(559)
G	4	side rails	hardwood	3/4	(19)	1 1/2	(38)	20 1/2	(521)
H	4	front and back rails	hardwood	3/4	(19)	1 1/2	(38)	15 1/8	(384)
J	1	door	melamine PB	5/8	(16)	17 3/4	(451)	30	(762)
DRAWERS									
K	2	upper drawer sides	melamine PB	5/8	(16)	4 3/8	(111)	22	(559)
L	2	upper drawer front and back	melamine PB	5/8	(16)	4 3/8	(111)	14 1/2	(368)
M	4	lower drawer sides	melamine PB	5/8	(16)	8 3/8	(213)	22	(559)
N	4	lower drawer fronts and backs	melamine PB	5/8	(16)	8 3/8	(213)	14 1/2	(368)
P	3	bottoms	melamine PB	5/8	(16)	15 3/4	(400)	22	(559)
Q	1	upper drawer face	melamine PB	5/8	(16)	8	(203)	17 3/4	(451)
R	2	lower drawer faces	melamine PB	5/8	(16)	10 15/16	(278)	17 3/4	(451)
S	1	countertop	MDF	3/4	(19)	25 1/2	(648)	60	(1524)

hardware & supplies

- 2" (51mm) PB screws
- 1 1/4" (32mm) PB screws
- 1" (25mm) PB screws
- 5/8" (16mm) PB screws
- melamine edge tape
- 12 L-brackets
- 4 handles
- 8 adjustable cabinet legs
- 5 sets 22" (559mm) drawer glides
- 2 hidden hinges and plates

SHOP *tip*

Melamine edge tape is paper based and coated with a heat-activated adhesive on one side. It can be easily applied with a household iron, but use an old iron because glue will transfer to the iron's plate. Edge trimming is the other part of the tape process, and you'll find many edge trimmers at all woodworking stores. Also, you'll need a fine file, preferably one called a laminate file, to smooth the cut edges of the tape.

1 One of the base cabinets will have two pullouts behind a door, and the other will be fitted with three drawers. However, both cabinet cases are constructed using identical techniques and panel sizes. Cut the four sides A, two bottoms B, two backs C and two rails D to the sizes indicated in the materials list. If the back C is cut square, the cabinet will be forced into square, so it's important to cut this panel accurately. Apply iron-on heat-activated adhesive melamine edge tape to the visible edges of all case panels. Tape should be applied to the front edges of the sides, front edges of the bottoms and the underside edge of the rails. The back's side edges will be visible if you have a cabinet side that's open to view, so apply melamine tape to those edges as well.

SHOP *tip*

If you want adjustable shelves in your base cabinets, you'll need to drill the two columns of shelf pin holes after you apply the melamine edge tape and before you assemble the cabinets. The cabinets I'm building will have drawers and pullouts, so shelf pin holes aren't required.

2 Both cases can be built at the same time. Join the sides A to the bottoms B, using 2" particleboard screws at 6" centers. Glue is not required for melamine particleboard joinery.The lower face of the bottom board is flush with the bottom edges of the side boards. Be sure to always drill a 1⁄8" pilot hole and a small counterbore for the particleboard screws.

3 The backs on the base cabinets are attached with 2" PB screws in pilot holes and follow a specific method. First, make sure you've cut the back C square. Then align the top edge of the back C to the top edge of the sides A, being sure the outside edge is flush with the outside face of the side boards. Install a 2" PB screw in one corner, then repeat the process in the other top corner. Next, repeat the same procedure and fasten the bottom two corners to the bottom B. Finally, install screws between the corners at 6" on center. Follow these steps when installing backs on base cabinets and the case will be correctly aligned and square.

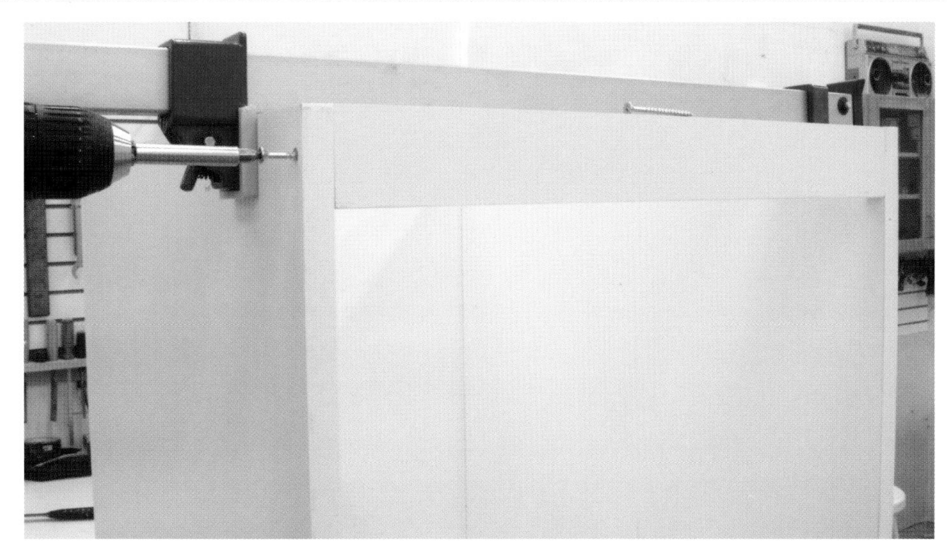

4 The rail D is the same width as the bottom B, which means the sides will be parallel. The rail is only 2" high, so it's secured with one 2"-long PB screw in the center of each end. It's wise to stay 1" away from any PB panel end to avoid splitting the material. The rail will be further supported in the next step. First, orient the rail so that the melanine edge tape is facing toward the bottom of the cabinet. Then, align the rail's top edge with the top ends of the sides. The rail face is flush with the side's front edges. Install the PB screws.

5 Install metal L-brackets between each end of the rail's rear face and a side. Use ⅝"-long screws to secure the brackets. Also, attach a bracket along the top edge of the rail, both sides and the back. These brackets will be used to secure the countertop.

6 Install four plastic adjustable legs (see the construction notes for options) on each base unit. Set the front legs back 3" to provide proper kick space when someone is standing in front of this cabinet. Position the legs, whenever possible, with the flange under the side's or back's edges. This leg placement will transfer loads from the countertop, through the vertical panels, into the legs and onto the floor. These legs are rated at a 600-pound load per leg, so they are strong enough for just about any application.

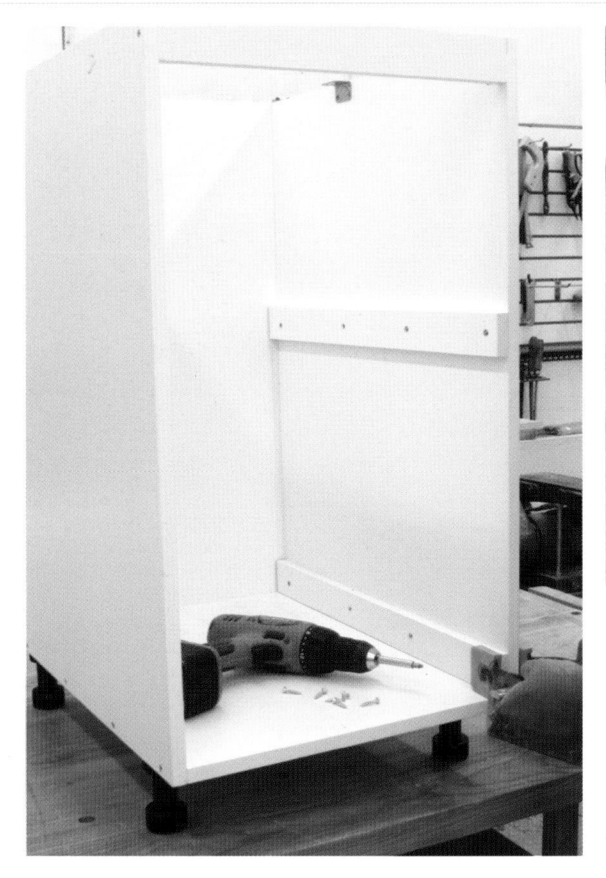

7 The cabinet on the right in my setup will be fitted with two pullouts behind a full-height door. Normally, pullouts and drawer boxes are 1" narrower than the cabinets inside width, using most drawer glide hardware. However, pullouts behind doors need extra clearance to travel past the door hinges. A spacer cleat must be installed on the hinge side. This base unit has one door, with hinges attached to the right side panel, so I will need one spacer cleat on the right for each pullout. The cleats E are 5⁄8"-thick melamine PB with all visible edges covered with edge tape. Secure the cleats to the side panel with 1"-long PB screws in piloted countersunk holes.

8 My pullouts are constructed using a melamine PB panel and hardwood rails. Refer to the construction notes at the end of this project for more options. The pullouts are 1" narrower than the interior cabinet width, including the spacer thickness, which reduces the width. The distance from spacer to side panel inside the cabinet is 16 1⁄8", so my pullout must be 15 1⁄8" wide to mount most drawer glide hardware. The depth equals the 22"-long glides I will be installing. Apply melamine edge tape to all visible edges of the pullout tray F. Use 1 1⁄4"-long PB screws to attach rails G and H from the underside of the pullout.

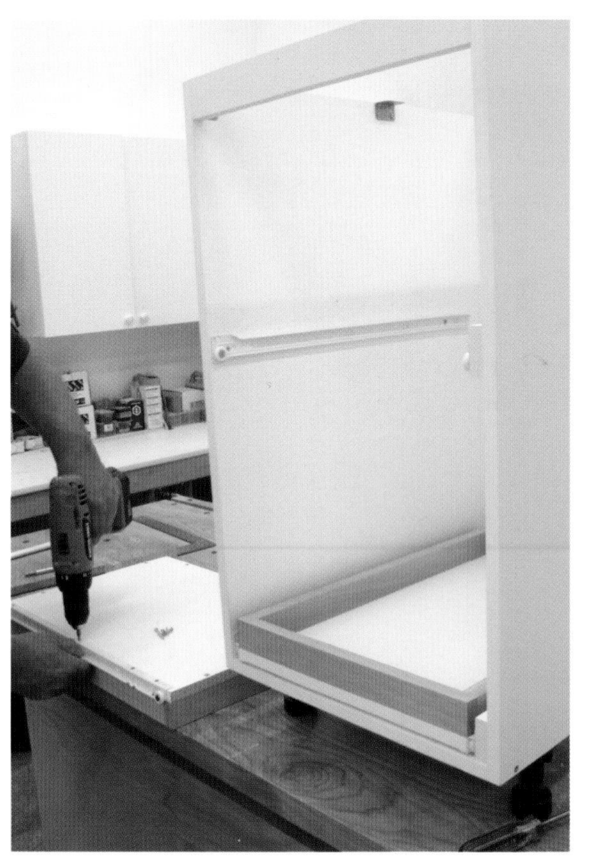

9 The simplest way to install drawer glides is to draw a line that's 90° to the cabinet's front edge. Use a carpenter's square to draw a center line for the screws and follow the manufacturer's installation instructions.

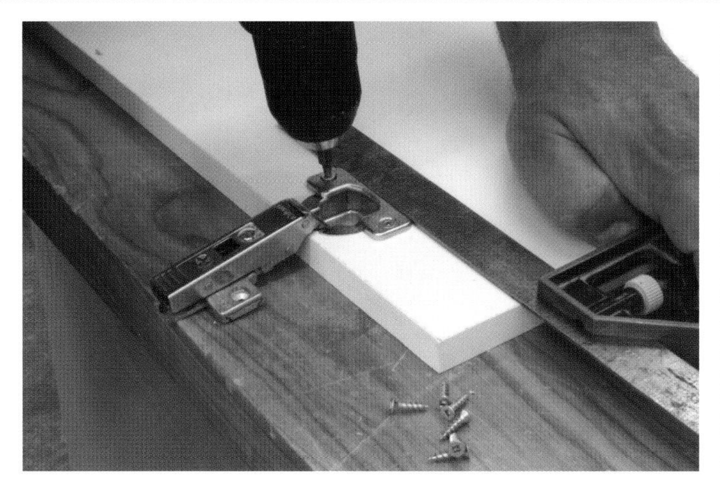

10 The door is 1" less than the cabinet case height at 30". It's 1" greater in width than the cabinet's interior width at 17¾". Cut the door to size, apply edge tape to all four edges and drill two 35mm-diameter holes ⅛" from the door's edge. The hinge holes are drilled 4" on center from each end. Mount the hinge and plate to the door, being sure to align the hinge arm at 90° to the door's edge.

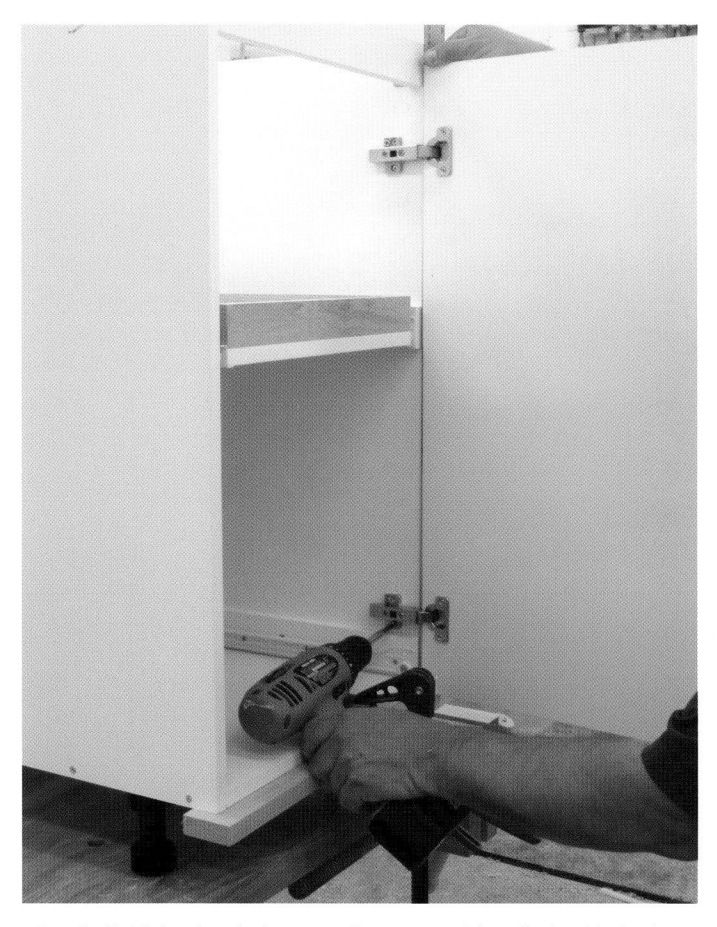

11 Hold the door in its normally open position, flush with the bottom board, and place a ⅛"-thick spacer between the cabinet's front edge and door's rear edge. Drive ⅝"-long PB screws through the hinge plate holes, into the cabinet's side, to secure the door. This installation procedure will quickly and accurately mount cabinet doors using hidden hinges. Install a door handle and cover the screw heads with plastic or self-adhesive cover caps. This completes the right-side unit construction.

SHOP *tip*

Drawer face heights, plus the 1⁄16" gap between them, should equal the height of cabinet doors in the same project. A three-drawer base, like the one being built in this project, should have a combined door face and gap height of 30" to equal the door height.

Decide on the height of each drawer face based on your requirements. The project unit has two 10 15⁄16"-high lower drawer faces and one 8"-high upper drawer face, as well as two 1⁄16"-high gaps. The total height of the faces and gaps is 30". The lower drawer boxes are 2" less in height than their drawer faces; the upper box is 3" less in height than its drawer face. This cabinet requires two 9"-high (8 15⁄16") lower drawer boxes and one 5"-high upper drawer box. Drawer boxes, like pullouts using standard drawer glides, are normally 1" narrower than the interior cabinet width. However, check the installation specifications of your hardware before cutting the box panels.

12 Cut drawer parts K, L, M, N and P to the sizes indicated in the materials list. Apply iron-on edge tape to all visible edges. Attach the sides K and M to the fronts and backs L and N, using 2"-long PB screws in piloted holes. The bottoms P are installed using 2" screws as well. Attach the bottoms by aligning and securing one corner at a time. After all four corners are aligned and secure, install screws between the corners at 6" on center.

13 Install the three drawer box cabinet glides at the bottom and at 11" and 22" above the top face of the bottom B. Drawer glide position equals the drawer box height plus 2" (9" + 2" = 11") above the bottom board's top surface. Use a carpenter's square to draw a reference line for the screw holes 90° to the cabinet's front edge. Attach the drawer box runners and test fit the drawers.

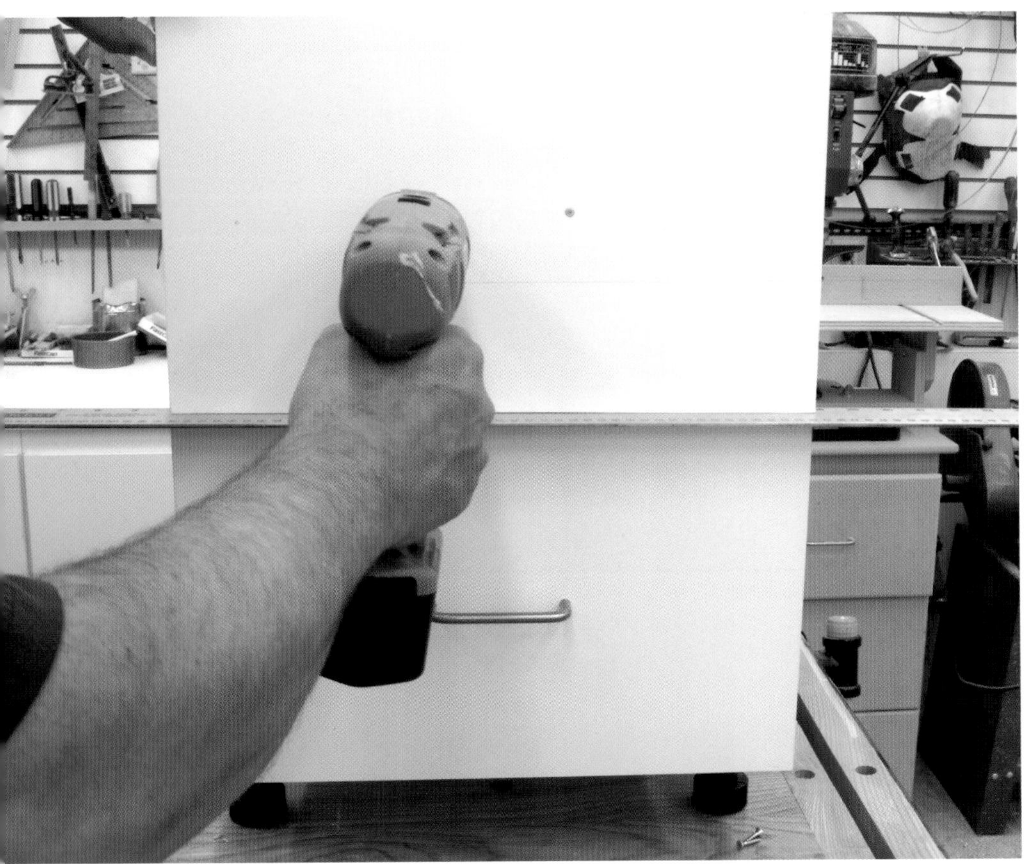

14 Cut and apply edge tape to the three drawer faces Q and R. The face height has already been determined, and the width is the same as cabinet doors at 1" greater than the cabinet's interior width. Drawer faces can be accurately installed by first drilling holes for the handles or knobs. The holes are drilled in the drawer faces only, not the drawer box at this point. Hold the lower drawer face R in place, flush with the lower edge of the cabinet bottom B and equally spaced on the cabinet sides A, and drive 1½"-long PB screws into the drawer box through the handle holes. The drawer face is now securely anchored to the box in the proper position. Drive 1"-long PB screws through the drawer box into the back of the drawer face. Next, place a 1⁄16"-thick spacer between the bottom and middle drawer faces. Repeat the steps for the middle and top faces. Once the drawer faces are secured, remove the temporary screws in the handle holes, drill through the drawer box and use machine screws to mount the handles.

15 The countertop is cut from a sheet of 3/4"-thick MDF. Refer to the construction notes for more countertop material options. Cut the top S to size and use a 1/4"-radius roundover bit to ease the top and bottom edges. Leave any edges that will be against a wall square. Place the top on both base units and use 5/8"-long PB screws through the L-brackets to attach the top. Don't use any adhesives when installing the countertop so it can be replaced if necessary.

construction NOTES

I've used plastic adjustable cabinet legs for this project because they are ideal for workshop cabinets. The legs are adjustable, unaffected by liquids and can support a great deal of weight. A fixed base, built using melamine PB or any other sheet materials, can also be used if desired.

The pullouts are melamine PB with hardwood rails as detailed in the construction steps. However, the rails can be made with melamine PB, plywood or any other sheet material you have in the shop. A few commercial options are available for the rails, such as plastic or metal systems, but these tend to be more expensive.

A wide variety of countertop options is available, like the 3/4" MDF I used, plywood, melamine PB or even solid-wood tops. The choice depends on your application and intended use for the workstation. Particleboard or plywood with solid-wood edges and a covering of high-pressure laminate (HPL) is another option if you need a fancier top. Standard countertop depth is normally 1 1/2" deeper than the base cabinet depth, and the length can be any dimension as long as the top is properly supported.

Cabinet width can be changed to suit your needs and can be as large as 36" wide. The depth is typically 24", not including the door thickness, but that isn't a fixed rule. Change the cabinet width to suit your requirements and follow the same assembly procedures as detailed in the project. Side panel dimensions are the same as shown, but the bottom, back and rail width will change based on the cabinet size. For example, a 30"-wide base will have two side panels at 23 3/8" x 31", one bottom at 23 3/8" x 28 3/4", a back at 30" x 31", and a rail measuring 2" high x 28 3/4" long using 5/8" sheet stock. If you prefer to work with 3/4" stock, change the panel dimensions accordingly.

These simple and versatile cabinets can be modified to suit any situation. They're easy to build and sturdy enough to support any table-mounted woodworking machine.

carpenter's toolbox

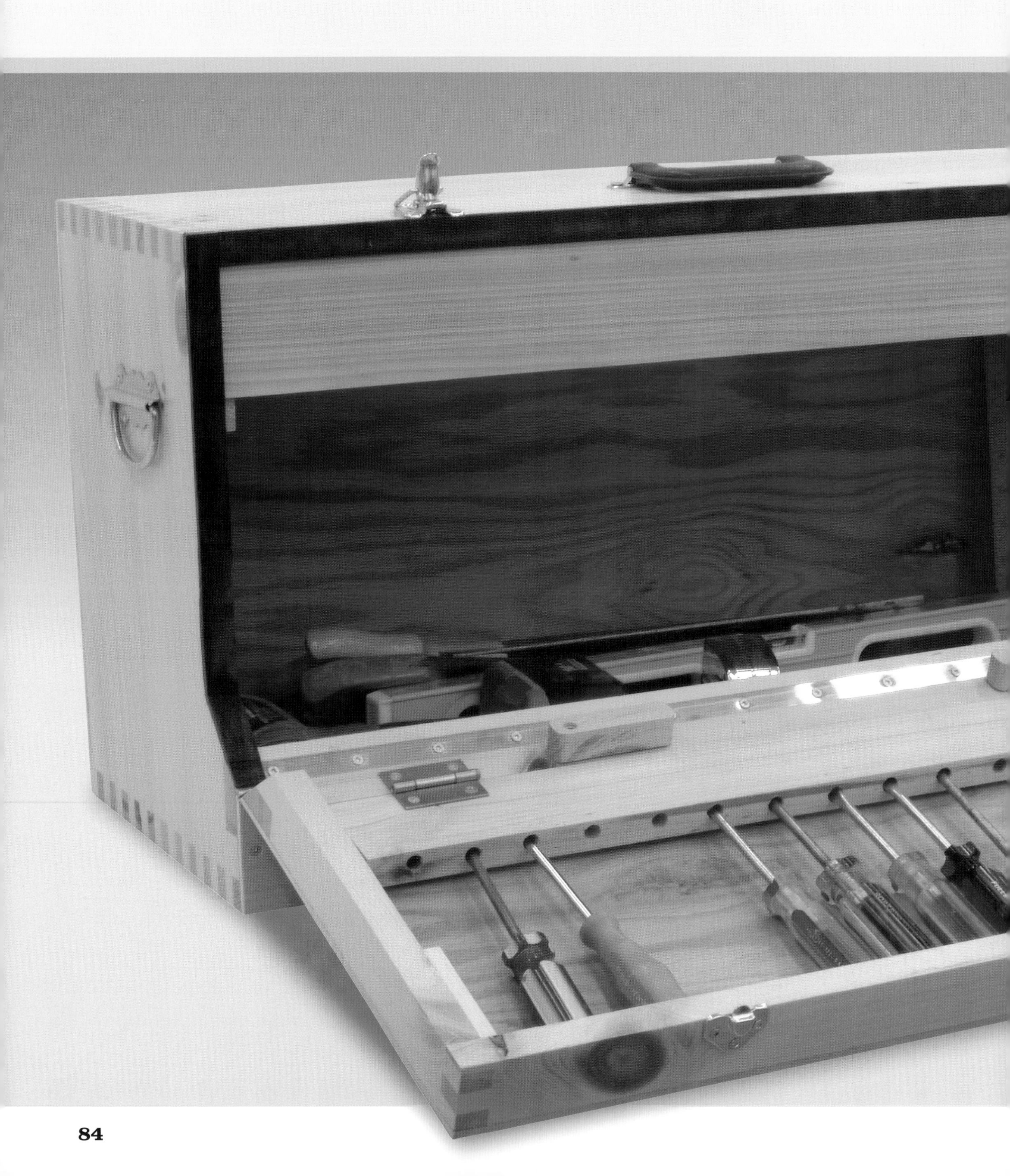

PROJECT

This is a great toolbox that's loaded with features and has plenty of storage room. However, before you start this project there are some issues that should be considered.

I decided to use knotty pine for my toolbox. It's light, inexpensive and easy to machine. However, I knew that I would have to accept a certain amount of wood tear-out when I cut the finger joints. No matter how much care you take or how sharp your cutting tools are, or even if you back up all the cuts with scrap lumber, soft pine will tear a little. There was a little damage when I cut my joints, but I was able to repair or hide most of the problem areas.

If, like me, you don't mind a few less-than-perfect cuts in exchange for the light weight and low cost of pine, then use the softwoods. But if you want perfection in your joinery, use a hardwood when building your toolbox. The choice is yours.

This project is all about box-building using glued-up solid wood and box joints, or as they are often called, finger joints. The sidebar at the end of the chapter details a simple jig you can make for your saw. As I mentioned in an earlier chapter, you should invest in a good carbide-tipped stacked dado blade for your table saw because this is another of its many uses. Give me a table saw with a dado blade and I can build anything.

A carpenter's toolbox can be used to carry hand tools and small electric tools to a work site. The box can be configured in many ways, so think about the tools you travel with most often and customize the interior space to suit your requirements. The large compartment can be used for cordless drills and sanders; the drawer will store chisels and hardware; and the door rack will organize all the screwdrivers you'll ever need on any job site.

Finally, don't be intimidated by the solid-wood glue-up procedures or box joinery. Both are basic woodworking techniques that are not difficult to master. The box joint is used in hundreds of applications and will open the door to many interesting projects. It's sometimes called a poor man's dovetail, but it's a strong, good-looking joint that's used every day in woodshops.

You don't need an expensive jointer or planer to edge-dress solid wood for panels. Acceptable low-cost alternatives are available and I'll detail the options in this project. If you don't need a carpenter's toolbox, there's sure to be a woodworker in your family who would really appreciate this project as a gift.

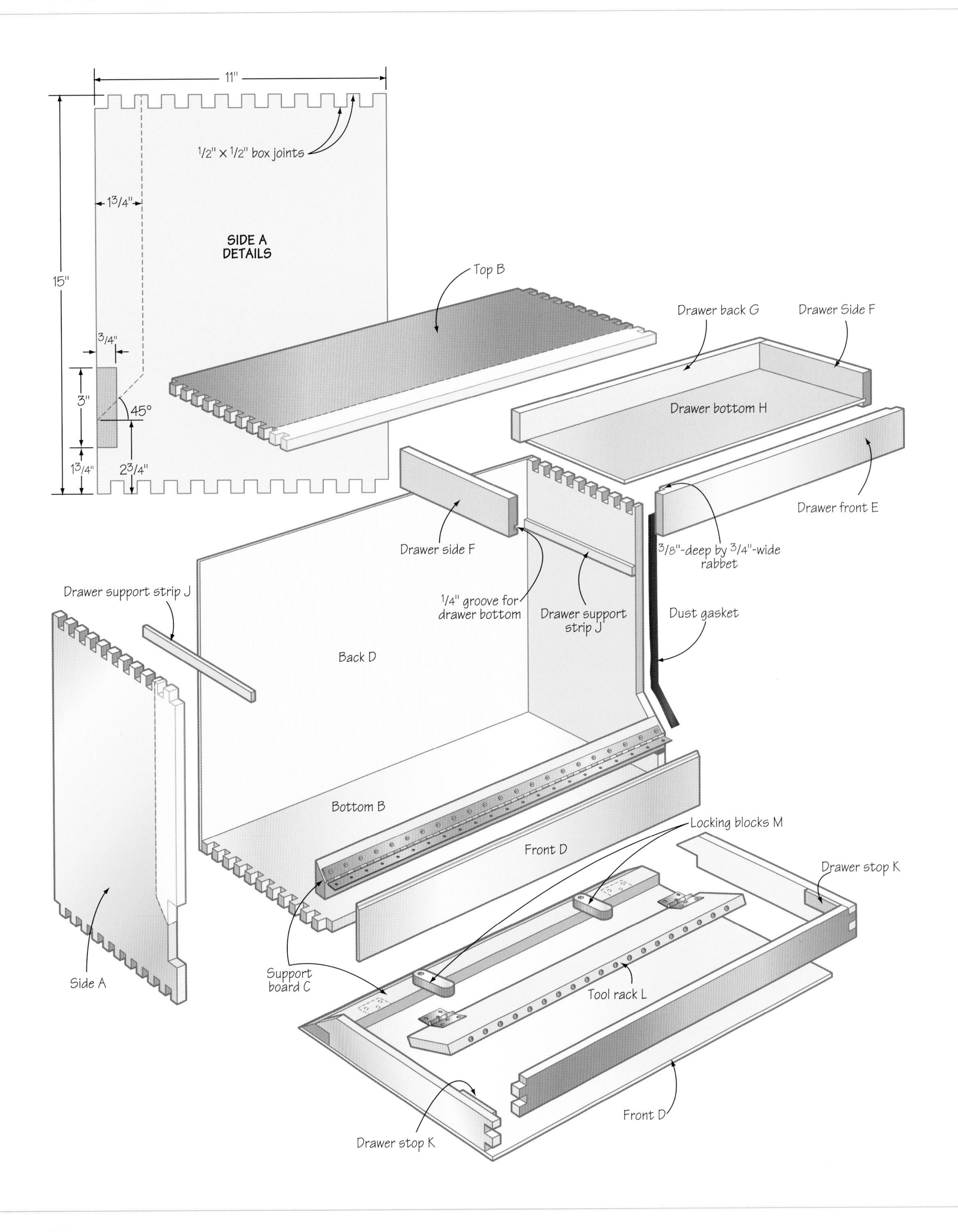
11"
1/2" x 1/2" box joints
1 3/4"
SIDE A DETAILS
15"
3/4"
3"
45°
1 3/4"
2 3/4"
Top B
Drawer back G
Drawer Side F
Drawer bottom H
Drawer front E
Drawer side F
3/8"-deep by 3/4"-wide rabbet
Drawer support strip J
1/4" groove for drawer bottom
Drawer support strip J
Dust gasket
Back D
Bottom B
Locking blocks M
Front D
Drawer stop K
Side A
Support board C
Tool rack L
Front D
Drawer stop K

inches (millimeters)

REFERENCE	QUANTITY	PART	STOCK	THICKNESS	(mm)	WIDTH	(mm)	LENGTH	(mm)
A	2	sides	solid wood	$^3/_4$	(19)	11	(279)	15	(381)
B	2	top and bottom	solid wood	$^3/_4$	(19)	11	(279)	30	(762)
C	1	support board	solid wood	$^3/_4$	(19)	3	(76)	30	(762)
D	2	front and back	veneer ply	$^1/_4$	(6)	15	(381)	30	(762)
E	1	drawer front	solid wood	$^3/_4$	(19)	3	(76)	$28^1/_2$	(724)
F	2	drawer sides	solid wood	$^3/_4$	(19)	3	(76)	$7^7/_8$	(200)
G	1	drawer back	solid wood	$^3/_4$	(19)	$2^1/_2$	(64)	$28^1/_2$	(724)
H	1	drawer bottom	veneer ply	$^1/_4$	(6)	$8^5/_8$	(219)	$27^3/_4$	(705)
J	2	drawer support strips	solid wood	$^3/_8$	(10)	$^3/_4$	(19)	9	(229)
K	2	drawer stops	solid wood	$^3/_8$	(10)	$^3/_4$	(19)	3	(76)
L	1	tool rack	solid wood	$^3/_4$	(19)	$2^1/_2$	(64)	28	(711)
M	2	locking blocks	solid wood	$^3/_4$	(19)	$^3/_4$	(19)	3	(76)

hardware & supplies

	glue
	$^1/_2$" (13mm) screws
	$^3/_4$" (19mm) brass screws
	1" (25mm) brass screws
	$1^1/_4$" (32mm) screws
	$1^1/_2$" (38mm) screws
	brad nails
2	3" (76mm) brass butt hinges
4	rubber feet
	30" (762mm) piano hinge
2	chest handles
1	luggage handle
4	$^1/_4$" (6mm) machine bolts, nuts and washers
2	draw catches
	4' (1219mm) $^3/_{16}$"-thick x $^3/_4$"-wide (5mm x 19mm) weather stripping

1 The first step is to edge-join enough solid wood to yield the side, top and bottom panels A and B. The edges of each board must be straight to achieve maximum contact when the boards are held together. They can be joined with glue or with glue and biscuits, as I'm doing. Either method is fine. If you don't have a jointer, you can have the lumberyard prepare the boards. However, a well-tuned table saw, with a sharp blade, will cut edges that are acceptable for this type of joinery. Be sure your saw fence is parallel to the saw blade and the blade is sharp. Cut one edge of the board, then flip it over so the cut edge is against the fence and cut the opposite side. Try to maintain an even steady speed when feeding the boards through the saw blade, removing small amounts on each pass. You may have to repeat this step one or two times, but you will get edges that can be joined. Now, edge-join the boards using biscuits and glue or glue only. Clamp the panels together until the glue sets.

2 Cut the sides A, top and bottom B, and support board C to the sizes listed in the materials list. Arrange the panels so they form the box shape and mark the front face of each board. Use matching numbers on each adjoining face to permit easy assembly once the fingers have been cut.

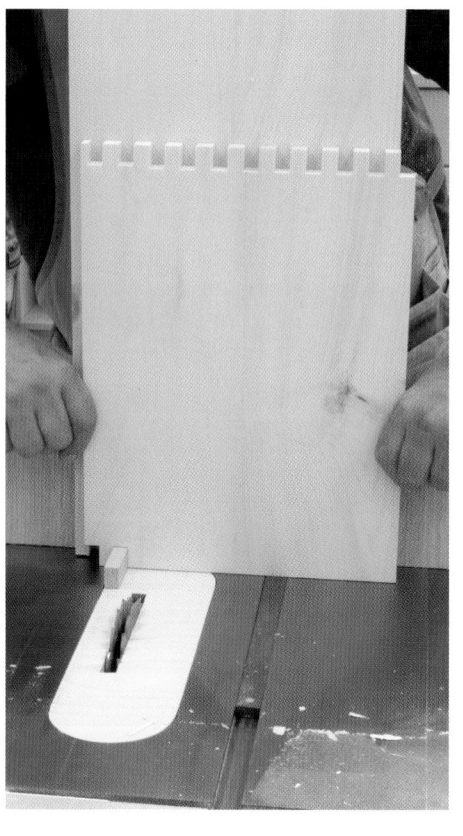

3 Use the jig and procedures described in the construction notes sidebar at the end of the chapter to cut the panels. Place the panel faces toward each other when cutting to reduce wood tear-out. I'm using a ½"-wide dado blade setting, which will cut ½"-wide notches and fingers.

4 Dry fit the box joints and mark the front edges. Take the joints apart and cut a notch on the front edges of the sides A for support board C. This support spans the two sides and will provide a backing for the front plywood panel after the door opening has been cut. The notch is ¾" deep, begins 1¾" from the bottom edge of each side panel, and is 3" wide.

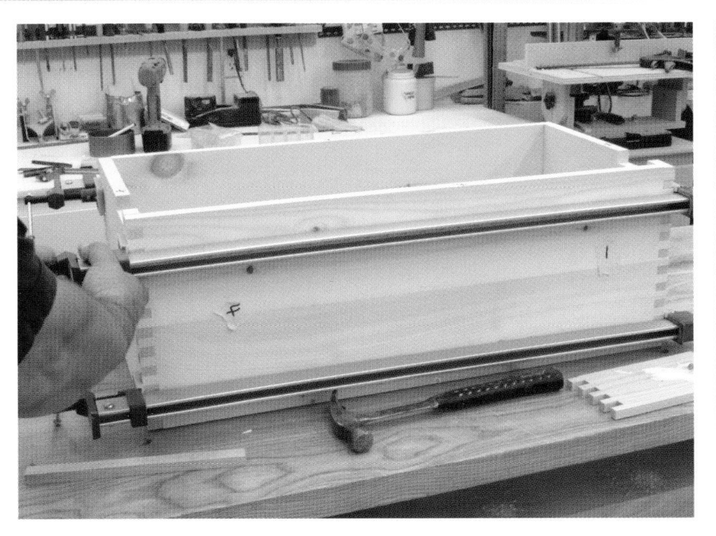

5 Coat the fingers and slots with glue, then assemble the box. Clamp the joints, making sure the corners are 90° by checking them with a square and moving them into alignment if necessary. Leave the clamps in place until the adhesive cures.

6 Apply glue to both side board notches and install support board C. Use clamps to hold it in place until the glue dries. Don't use any nails or screws on this joint, because the door-opening cut will be made through this board.

7 The front and back panels D are 1/4"-thick veneer plywood that matches the solid wood. Cut them to the size listed in the materials list and attach them to the box, using glue and 3/4"-long brass screws. Start the screws 1 1/2" from each corner and space them about 5" to 6" apart.

8 To cut the box apart, set the angle of your table saw blade to 45°. The cut will be made through the support board C beginning 2 3/4" from the bottom of the box. The angle is toward the box top. The cut depth (or length) depends on the amount of rise on your blade. My cut is 1 3/4" deep, measured from the front of the toolbox. The blade should have a 1/8"-wide kerf (blade thickness) to remove enough material for the dust gasket. Push the box through the saw blade.

9 Extend the inner and outer angle cut lines, using a pencil and carpenter's square, to the box top. Set the table saw blade back to 90° and raise it above the tabletop as high as possible. Carefully align the saw fence so the box will be guided through the blade between the pencil lines on each side of the the angle cut. Push the box through the saw blade.

10 Place 1⁄8"-thick spacers in the top saw kerf and clamp the door. Use two more clamps to secure the toolbox to your workbench. Verify that both saw cuts on each side are accurately joined with pencil lines. Use a sharp handsaw to complete the door cut between the two table saw cuts on each side. The table saw blade kerf will be thicker than a handsaw kerf, so a little sanding will be required to smooth both cuts.

11 Install a few more 3⁄4"-long brass screws above and below the front face cut to further secure the front D to the support board.

12 Cut all the drawer parts to the sizes given in the materials list. The drawer box is 9" deep by 28 1⁄2" wide by 3" high. Use a dado or standard blade on the table saw to form a 3⁄8"-deep by 3⁄4"-wide rabbet cut on the back face at each end of the drawer front E.

13 The two drawer sides F and front E need a $\frac{1}{4}$"-wide by $\frac{3}{8}$"-deep groove on the inside face to receive the bottom H. This groove begins $\frac{1}{4}$" above the bottom edge of each board.

14 Apply glue to the front board's rabbets and attach the sides with 1"-long brass screws. The grooves on the sides and front must align to receive the bottom board.

15 The drawer back G is $2\frac{1}{2}$" high, so the $\frac{1}{4}$"-thick bottom H can be attached to its bottom edge. Attach the back G to the ends of the sides F with glue and $1\frac{1}{2}$"-long screws. Slide the bottom panel into the grooves and secure it in place with a few brad nails driven into the back G.

16 The drawer support strips J are small strips of wood that are glued and screwed to the toolbox sides. Place the drawer box in the toolbox to locate and install these supports.

17 Attach the drawer stops K with glue and $\frac{3}{4}$" brass screws. They are located at the top of the door and in line with the drawer box. They will keep the drawer box closed when the toolbox door is closed.

19 Following the finish application, install feet so the box bottom won't be in contact with the floor. I'm using small rubber feet that are attached with $\frac{3}{4}$"screws and are available at most hardware stores.

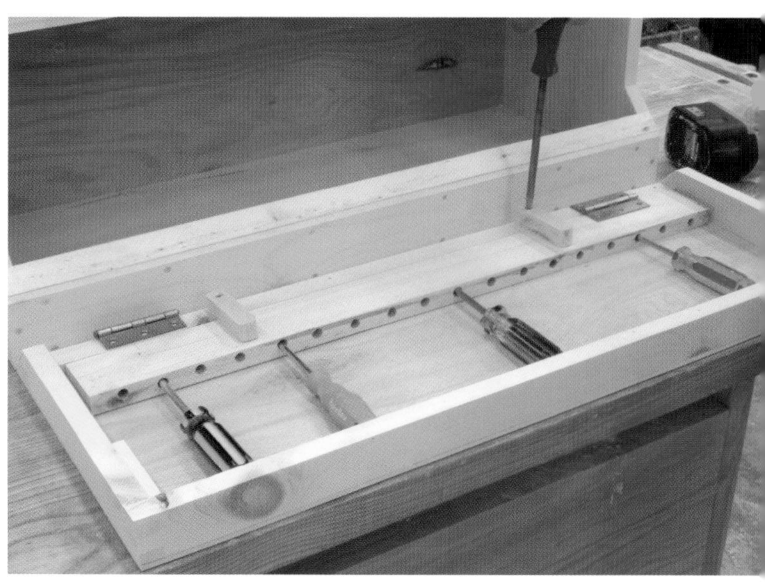

18 The tool holder is optional, but it's a great addition to this box. The hole diameter in the rack should be sized for the type of tools that will be stored. Mine will be used for screwdrivers of all sizes, so I've drilled a series of $\frac{3}{8}$"-diameter holes. The tool rack L is held in place by two small butt hinges. It's held tight to the door with wood locking blocks M that can be turned to lock or release the rack. However, don't install the rack, hinges, locking blocks or any other hardware at this point, because it's an ideal time to apply a finish to the toolbox. I'm using three coats of polyurethane to protect my toolbox.

20 The door is attached to the toolbox using a 30"-long by $\frac{1}{2}$"-wide piano hinge. Note that you can only use $\frac{1}{2}$"-long screws to secure the door part of the hinge, as longer screws will break through the front panel. Align the door face to the box front panel and the top to the toolbox top board. There should be a constant $\frac{1}{8}$"-wide gap between the toolbox case and door.

21 Attach the tool rack using small butt hinges. The wood locking blocks can also be attached using 1¼"-long screws.

22 Each side of the toolbox will have a chest handle installed that's 3½" below the top surface of the box. I've used ¾"-long screws to attach my handles, but I suggest you use through-bolts and nuts if you plan to carry a lot of tools. You can also purchase larger chest handles, which are more comfortable, if they will be the primary method used to lift the toolbox.

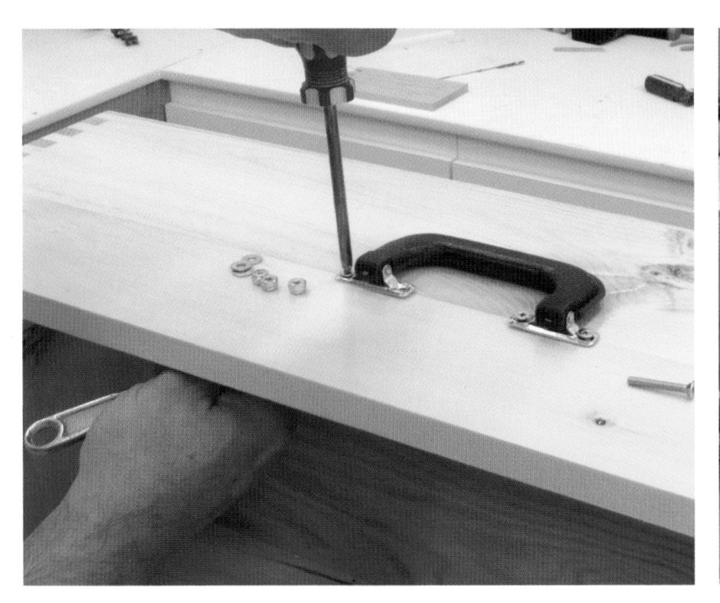

23 A luggage handle can be installed on the top center of the toolbox for one-handed carrying. Use through-bolts with nuts instead of screws, because this handle will carry the total weight.

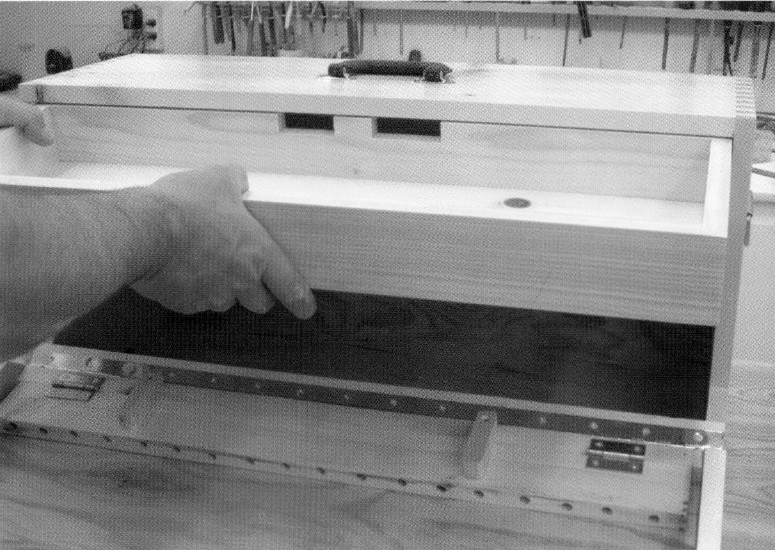

24 The drawer back G must be notched to clear the nuts on the luggage handle. Use a handsaw and chisel to cut the notches.

Building a Finger-Joint Jig

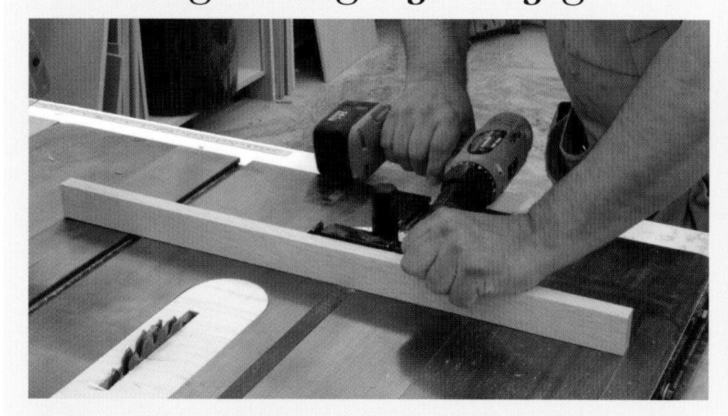

STEP 1 Attach a long 1" x 2" extension on your table saw miter fence. It will be used to support the finger-joint indexing panel.

STEP 2 Clamp an indexing panel, which is about 8" high and 24" long, to the extension board on your miter fence. This tall indexing panel will help support large boards as they are pushed through the dado blade. Once secured, cut through the indexing panel. I am setting up and testing this jig with a ½"-wide dado blade.

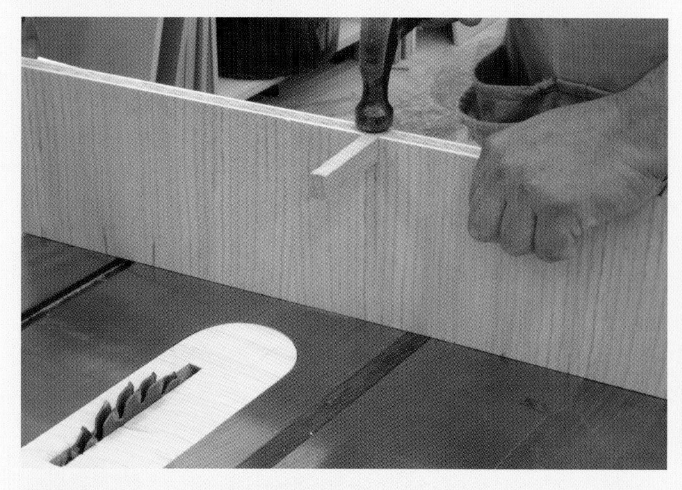

STEP 3 Cut a wood indexing pin, which equals the cut width, and glue it in the notch on the panel.

STEP 4 Use a loose indexing pin, which also is the same width as the notch, to set the fixed indexing pin ½" away from the dado blade. Clamp the indexing board securely to the miter fence extension.

STEP 5 Cut the two boards to be joined together. Hold the rear board tightly to the fixed indexing pin, and set the front board away from the fixed pin, using the loose indexing pin as a guide. Remove the loose indexing pin and make the first cut.

STEP 6 The second cut is made with the rear board notch over the indexing pin and the front board tight to the pin. Make the remaining cuts by moving the notches over the pin until all fingers and slots have been formed. If the test joint is loose, move the indexing panel so the fixed pin is slightly farther away from the blade. If the fingers are too wide for the notches, move the fixed indexing pin toward the blade. Be careful when moving the index board, because it doesn't take very much pin movement to dramatically change the finger and slot width.

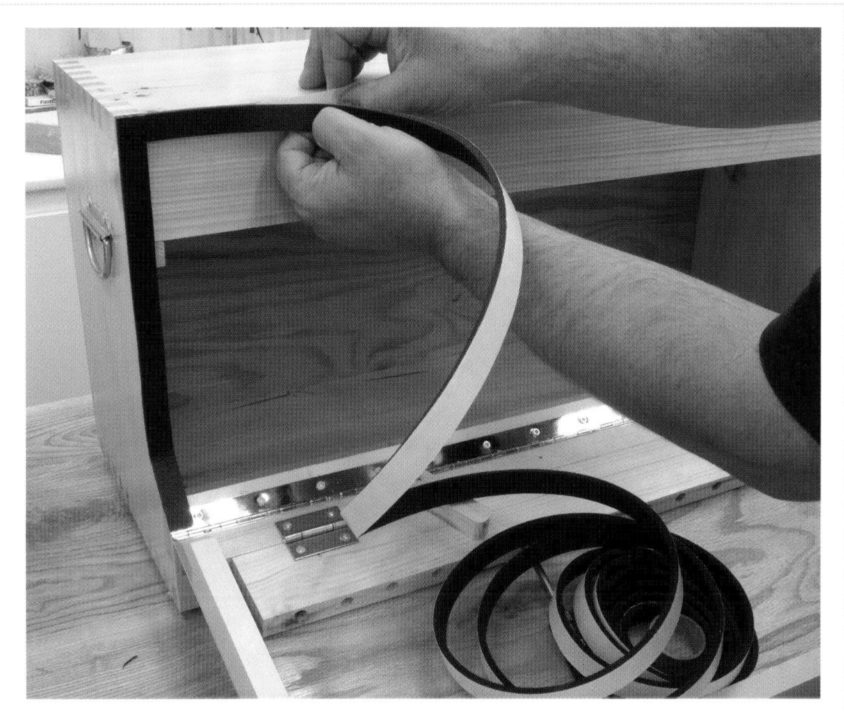

25 The gasket I'm using is called heavy-duty foam tape weather-stripping and is available in hardware stores. This material is commonly used to weather-strip doors and is self-adhesive and waterproof. The size that seems to work best is 3⁄16" thick by 3⁄4" wide. The tape will form a gasket that should keep most of the dirt and sawdust from entering the toolbox.

26 The final step is to install two draw catches to hold the door closed. Use 3⁄4"-long screws and space the catches evenly on the box. You can also add a lock at this point if you need added security for your toolbox.

construction NOTES

So many options and changes can be made when designing your toolbox. The first choice, as mentioned at the start of this project, relates to the type of wood used. Hardwood will machine better, and you will have less tear-out on the fingers and slots compared to softwood. However, softwood is less expensive, lighter and easier to cut, but be aware of the results.

The tool rack can be customized to hold a lot of different tools. You might find it more useful to store marking tools or chisels in the rack, so drill and space the holes to suit your needs. Alternately, you might find the door space more valuable for tools like levels and squares, which means you'll need to design another style of holder.

Hardware is a major part of this project. If you plan to move this toolbox a great deal, or use it on a job site every day, you should purchase heavy-duty chest handles, draw catches and luggage handles. Use through-bolts and nuts in place of screws when attaching the heavier hardware. The chest handles I've used are more decorative than practical, and I wouldn't want to be lifting the box using these handles on a daily basis. I did see large, comfortable, industrial-style chest handles that would be much better suited for everyday use.

This toolbox has one 3"-high drawer but can have two 2"-high drawers or any combination of sizes. Look at what you plan to carry in your toolbox and decide which drawer design is best suited to your needs.

I built a couple of boxes using a special, thin-kerf blade, so the door gap was almost eliminated. That's another option you may want, but I like the gasket feature, which should help to eliminate the dust and dirt that builds up in toolboxes.

Before you begin to build this toolbox, decide on the best overall size for your needs. It can be made larger or smaller with a few minor dimensional changes. If you need to carry large tools, such as framing squares, the box will have to be taller. The plans are flexible and can be altered to meet your needs.

carver's tool chest

PROJECT 11

I've always been interested in woodcarving, but haven't had the time or equipment to get started. This dedicated carver's tool chest is my way of getting motivated. Now that I have a special place for carving tools, I can begin putting everything together.

Those of you who carve wood know that a clean, well-organized storage cabinet is an important requirement. Dozens of knives, chisels, mallets and other tools must be within easy reach and kept in an area intended to protect the finely ground edges. It's not very productive, and often frustrating, when you have to spend valuable time looking for the right carving tool.

This chest is constructed using solid hardwood, with the exception of the top shelf, back and tray bottom boards. It has two 2"-high trays and two that are 3" high. The hinged top covers another storage compartment, so there should be enough room to meet most carvers' needs. The shallow, wide trays, as well as the upper compartment, will let you separate tools so they are easily seen and accessible.

There are hundreds of ways to build a tool chest; this project demonstrates one method. The top lid and side center panels are glued-up solid boards. I'll detail an easy way to make raised panels on a table saw so you won't need an expensive router or shaper to build this chest.

The trays glide on wooden runners, which was a common technique before modern hardware was available. The trays have solid-wood backs, fronts and sides, with grooves that allow them to travel along the wood glides. And because most carving tools are small and light, a simple veneer plywood drawer bottom is all that's needed.

Dedicated carvers will appreciate the features built into this chest. However, if you're like me and want to get started in carving, building this chest is a great beginning. I enjoyed building this project, and I'm sure you will as well.

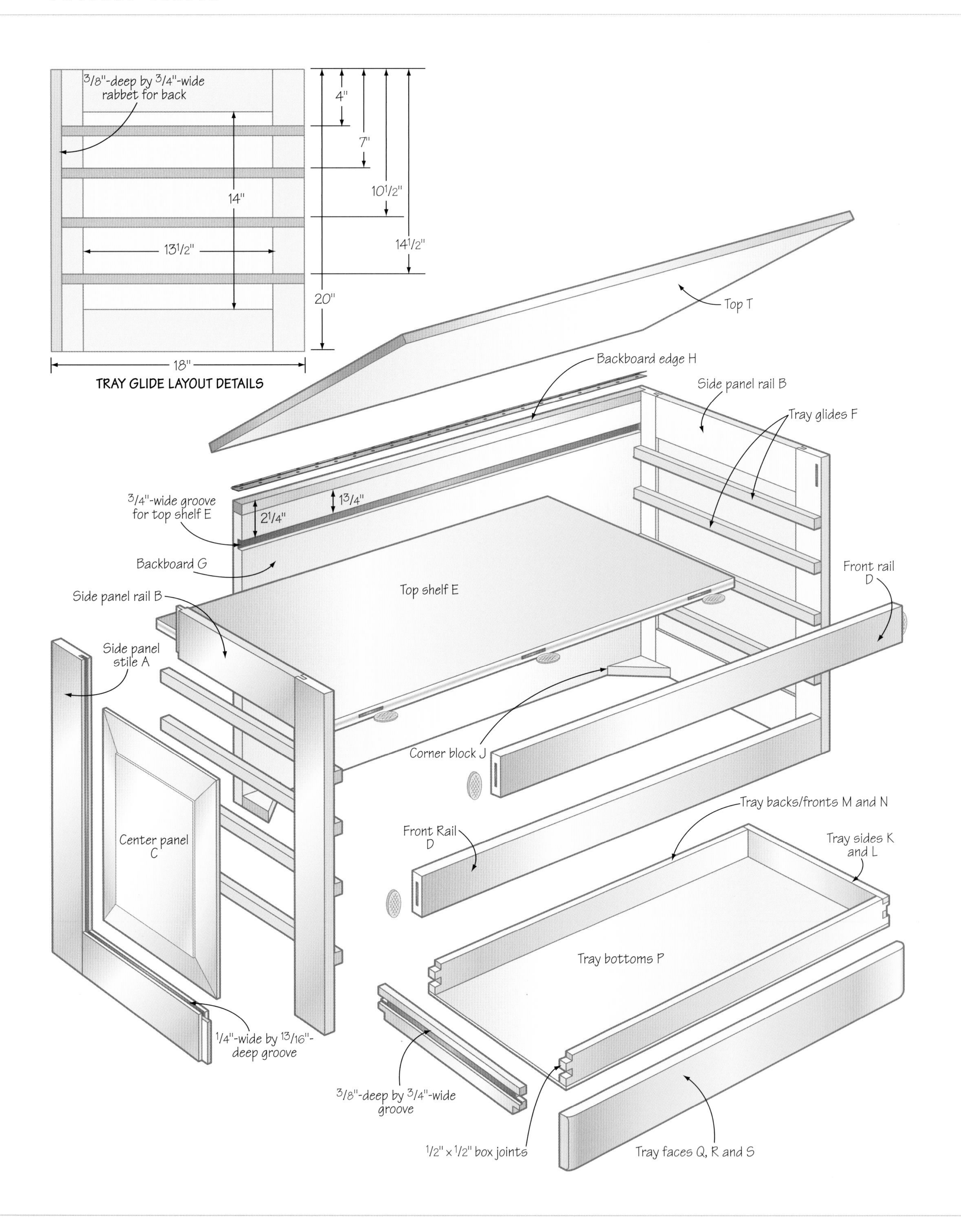

3/8"-deep by 3/4"-wide rabbet for back
4"
7"
10 1/2"
14 1/2"
14"
13 1/2"
20"
18"
TRAY GLIDE LAYOUT DETAILS
Top T
Backboard edge H
Side panel rail B
Tray glides F
3/4"-wide groove for top shelf E
1 3/4"
2 1/4"
Backboard G
Top shelf E
Front rail D
Side panel rail B
Side panel stile A
Corner block J
Tray backs/fronts M and N
Front Rail D
Tray sides K and L
Center panel C
Tray bottoms P
1/4"-wide by 13/16"-deep groove
3/8"-deep by 3/4"-wide groove
1/2" x 1/2" box joints
Tray faces Q, R and S

inches (millimeters)

REFERENCE	QUANTITY	PART	STOCK	THICKNESS	(mm)	WIDTH	(mm)	LENGTH	(mm)
A	4	side panel stiles	hardwood	3/4	(19)	2 1/4	(57)	20	(508)
B	4	side panel rails	hardwood	3/4	(19)	3	(76)	15	(381)
C	2	center panels	hardwood	3/4	(19)	15	(381)	15 1/2	(394)
D	2	front rails	hardwood	3/4	(19)	3	(76)	28	(711)
E	1	top shelf	veneer ply	3/4	(19)	16 7/8	(429)	28	(711)
F	8	tray glides	hardwood	3/8	(10)	11/16	(18)	17	(432)
G	1	back board	veneer ply	3/4	(19)	19 1/2	(495)	28 3/4	(730)
H	1	back board edge	hardwood	3/4	(19)	1/2	(13)	28 3/4	(730)
J	4	corner blocks	hardwood	3/4	(19)	3 1/2	(89)	3 1/2	(89)
K	4	upper tray sides	hardwood	3/4	(19)	2	(51)	17	(432)
L	4	lower tray sides	hardwood	3/4	(19)	3	(76)	17	(432)
M	4	upper backs and fronts	hardwood	3/4	(19)	2	(51)	27 15/16	(710)
N	4	lower backs and fronts	hardwood	3/4	(19)	3	(76)	27 15/16	(710)
P	4	tray bottoms	veneer ply	1/4	(6)	17	(432)	27 15/16	(710)
Q	2	top tray faces	hardwood	3/4	(19)	3 1/4	(83)	29 1/2	(749)
R	1	middle tray face	hardwood	3/4	(19)	4	(102)	29 1/2	(749)
S	1	bottom tray face	hardwood	3/4	(19)	4 1/2	(114)	29 1/2	(749)
T	1	top	hardwood	3/4	(19)	19	(483)	31 1/2	(800)

hardware & supplies

	glue
	No. 10 biscuits
	brad nails
	3/4" (19mm) screws
	1 1/4" (32mm) screws
1	29 1/2" (749mm) piano hinge
2	12" (305mm) lid chains
8	tray handles

1 Before you begin, glue up the solid-wood side center panels C and wood top T. They require time for the adhesive to set, so after joining and clamping, put them aside until needed. As discussed in project ten, you don't need a jointer to successfully glue up solid wood. Ask the lumberyard to prepare the boards, which many will do for a small fee. However, a well-tuned table saw with a sharp blade will cut edges that are acceptable for this type of joinery. Be sure your saw fence is parallel to the saw blade and the blade is sharp. Cut one edge of the board, then flip it over so the cut edge is against the fence and cut the opposite side. Try to maintain an even, steady speed when feeding the boards through the saw blade, removing small amounts on each pass. You may have to repeat this step one or two times, but you will get edges that can be joined. If you prefer, edge joinery can be successfully done using a hand plane specifically made to plane edges. A good plane can be a real asset to your solid-panel work, and it's a worthwhile investment. If you haven't got room for a power jointer, or don't appreciate the noise it generates, consider purchasing a hand plane. Edge-join the top panel T using glue and biscuits. However, the two center panels C must be edge-joined using only glue, because a lot of wood will be removed when the panels are raised, and a biscuit joint may be exposed.

2 Cut the side panel stiles A and rails B to the sizes indicated in the materials list. Use a table saw to form a $\frac{1}{4}$"-wide by $\frac{13}{16}$"-deep groove along one edge of each piece. To ensure the groove is centered on your $\frac{3}{4}$" stock, set the inside face of the saw blade $\frac{1}{4}$" away from the fence. Push the boards through the blade, then reverse the board and run it through the blade again. That process will center the groove, but a small strip of material may be left in the middle if your blade is less than $\frac{1}{8}$" thick. If that's the case, adjust the fence and run a cleaning pass in the center of each groove.

3 Each of the four rails B requires a $\frac{1}{4}$"-thick by $\frac{3}{4}$"-long tenon on both ends. These can be cut with a standard saw blade by making multiple passes over the blade or with a dado blade. Test the cuts on scrap material to be sure the tenons fit properly in the grooves.

4 Cut the two side center panels C to size. These panels will be raised on a table saw. First, lower the blade below the table surface and secure a strong board across its center 90° to the blade face. The best blade for this technique is a large-kerf (thick) rip blade. The miter slide can be used to align the guide board.

5 Begin with the blade $\frac{1}{32}$" above the table surface. Push all four sides of both center panels along the guide board and across the blade. Repeat the process, raising the blade $\frac{1}{32}$" after each series of passes, until the edges of the panels fit loosely into the stile and rail grooves. Be sure the panels can move freely inside the grooves to allow for expansion and contraction of the wood. Slow, steady passes across the blade will yield the best cuts and reduce sanding after the cuts have been completed. Use a push pad in the center of each panel so the panel won't tip as the edges get thinner.

6 Sand the panel edges and assemble both side panels, using glue on the tenons only. Clamp them securely until the glue sets up. The center panels should float in the grooves. Ensure the frames are square by measuring the diagonals. If the dimensions are the same, the panel is square.

7 Form a $\frac{3}{4}$"-wide by $\frac{3}{8}$"-deep rabbet on the rear inside face of each side panel. Use a dado blade on your table saw or a router with a $\frac{3}{4}$" straight-cutting bit along with a guide.

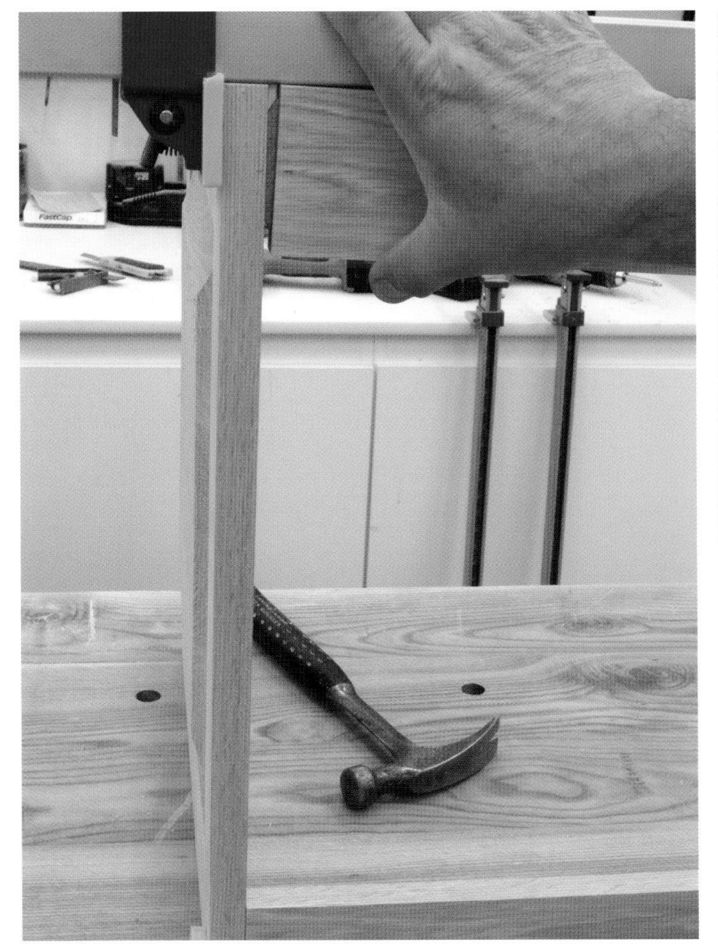

8 The two front rails D will be secured to the sides using biscuit joinery. Use No. 10 biscuits for this application because the No. 20 is too wide. Cut a biscuit slot on the center ends of each rail, and a slot in the side panels. The top rail is flush with the top edges of the side panels, and the bottom is flush with the lower ends. Once you have cut the biscuit slots, dry fit the parts but do not glue them at this point.

9 The top compartment's fixed shelf E is $16\frac{7}{8}$" deep. It will extend $\frac{3}{8}$" into the space for the rear rabbet cuts because it will be secured in a $\frac{3}{8}$"-deep groove on the backboard G. The bottom edge of this fixed shelf should be aligned with the bottom edge of the top rail. Turn the cabinet on its top edges and mark the position for three biscuit slots on the bottom face. Cut the slots in both top shelf E and upper front rail D. Check the fit, then take the case apart.

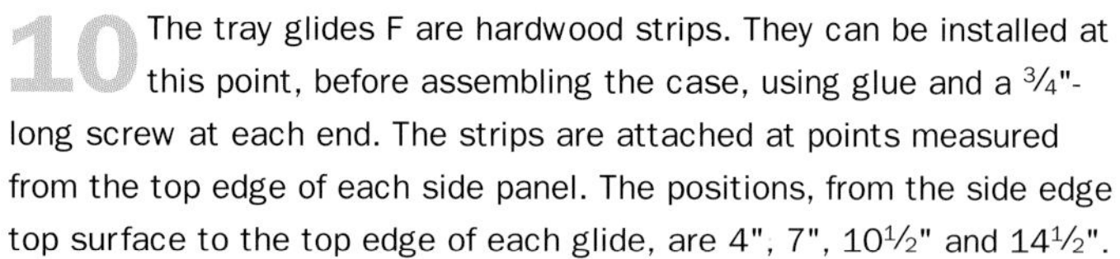

10 The tray glides F are hardwood strips. They can be installed at this point, before assembling the case, using glue and a 3/4"-long screw at each end. The strips are attached at points measured from the top edge of each side panel. The positions, from the side edge top surface to the top edge of each glide, are 4", 7", 10 1/2" and 14 1/2".

11 The case can now be assembled using glue on the biscuits and along both sides of the top shelf E. This shelf will be held more securely once its back edge is placed in the backboard's groove. When all the parts are properly aligned, clamp the case and wait until the adhesive cures.

12 The backboard is 20" high and is a combination of the back board edge strip H attached to the 3/4"-thick panel of veneer plywood G. Attach the hardwood strip to the top edge, using glue and brad nails. Cut a 3/4"-wide by 3/8"-deep groove in the backboard to receive the top shelf E. The groove's top edge is 2 1/4" below the top edge of the backboard with the hardwood strip in place. Put glue in the groove and on the rabbet cuts on each side panel. Install the backboard with the hardwood strip on the top edge and the fixed shelf E in the groove. Clamp the assembly or drive a few brad nails through the back face of the backboard to keep it secure.

13 Strengthen the bottom section of the case by installing four corner blocks J. Cut them on a 45° angle to size and attach them using glue and brad nails.

14 The trays are $\frac{1}{16}$" narrower than the cabinet's inside width. The sides, back and front boards are $\frac{3}{4}$" hardwood stock. I will detail the process used to make box joints for the corner joinery, but many other joints can be used. If you do decide to use a screw and butt joint, don't place the screws in the middle of the side boards, because grooves will be cut in the center. Cut parts K, L, M and N to size, then set up your $\frac{1}{2}$" box-cutting jig (see the sidebar "Building a Finger-Joint Jig" at the end of project ten). These are narrow boards, so use a square to make certain they are aligned 90° to the table saw top before cutting.

15 Each finger and slot for these box joints is $\frac{1}{2}$" wide. To properly interlock, the sides K and L are indexed differently than the fronts and backs M and N. Use the indexing pin to space the sides $\frac{1}{2}$" away from the fixed pin on each initial cut. The backs and fronts can be started tight to the fixed pin. That setup will align the fingers and notches correctly. Remember to orient the boards properly when cutting each end. To guarantee correct positioning, place a mark on the bottom edges of the 16 tray boards. Now, start all the cuts on both ends of each board with the mark facing the fixed pin.

16 Assemble the four trays with glue applied to all fingers and slots. Clamp the trays and measure the diagonals to ensure they are square. If the measurements are different, a slight twist or tap on the long side will equalize the measurements.

17 I want as much depth as possible in each tray. To achieve this, I'm using 1/4"-thick veneer plywood for the tray bottoms P. Nail and glue the tray bottoms P to the tray frame bottoms.

18 A 3/4"-wide groove is needed on both sides of each tray. They will fit over the tray glides F and should be centered on each side. If the cutting, assembly and measurements are correct, the grooves should all be 3/8" deep. However, that's not always the case, so I suggest you sneak up on the correct groove depth. The best tool to cut these grooves is a stacked dado blade on a table saw. Begin with a 1/4"-deep groove on each side and test fit the tray. If necessary, cut the grooves a little deeper to achieve the correct fit. The tray should be snug on the glides, without binding, because they will be fine-tuned and waxed after finishing until they slide smoothly.

19 The tray faces Q, R and S are the full cabinet width at 29½". Cut all four faces to the sizes indicated in the materials list and round over each front outside face with a 3/8"-radius roundover bit.

20 Attach the tray faces to the tray boxes using three 1¼"-long screws through the back side of the front boards. The easiest way to properly align the faces is to first drill the handle holes in the tray faces only. Then, using a 2½"-high spacer under the bottom face, drive screws through the handle holes into the tray box. Now that the face is securely attached to the tray box in the correct position, it can be slid open to install the 1¼" screws inside the tray. Remove the front screws and install the handles after completing the handle-hole drilling. Continue the installation process, moving up one face at a time with a 1/16"-thick spacer between tray faces.

21 The top T is a glued-up hardwood panel. It's installed flush with the backboard and extends 1" past the front and sides of the chest. Cut it to size and round over the top and bottom edges of the sides with a 3⁄8"-radius bit in a router. Leave the bottom, back edge square so there will be a straight edge to install the piano hinge. Mount the top with a 29½"-long by ½"-wide piano hinge. Set the nails that hold the wood edge strip on top of the backboard ¼" below the surface with a nail set punch. The hinge recess can be cut on the table saw by setting your blade ½" above the tabletop, and the fence-to-blade distance 1⁄8" smaller than the chest height.

22 Attach two 12"-long chains to the chest lid to limit its travel. Once the trays and lid are operating correctly, apply a finish.

construction *NOTES*

Many of my wood projects are built using red oak, and this one is no exception. However, any hardwood, or softwood for that matter, that's reasonably priced in your area can be used.

The most important design issue is the tray size, and the options are endless. Inventory the tools you want to store and change the tray sizes to suit your requirements. Also, the trays can be lined with felt to protect delicate carving knives or equipped with holders so your chisels and knives have a dedicated space.

This is a large tool chest, which may be sized correctly for many carvers, but it can be easily made smaller or larger if needed. The top can also be fitted with a lock if you want to secure expensive, and potentially dangerous, knives and fine carving tools. The trays may be a little more difficult to outfit with locks, with the exception of the top tray, which could easily be secured using the top rail.

When I researched this project, I came across many carving chests that did have tool holders. They were the half-circle type and typically held chisels. I didn't want to design the insert holders until I had all my carving tools because there are so many types and styles of handles on the market. I believe these holders should be customized for your tools, so that part of the project will be your design.

Finally, don't be intimidated by the box joints; you can use a number of other corner joints, like simple butt joints to build the trays. Remember to keep any hardware outside the ¾"-wide groove path that must be cut in each side board. You can also use dovetail joints for the tray corners if you feel confident using that method. Remember to apply a good coat of hard paste wax to the drawer glides once in a while, and they will provide years of reliable service.

mobile tool chest

PROJECT 

How do you build a mobile toolbox to suit everyone's needs? That's the question I faced when designing this project. I soon realized that I couldn't meet everyone's requirements. A woodworker who likes building deck and outdoor projects has very different tool storage requirements than someone who does a lot of interior trim carpentry.

I decided to make a sectional mobile chest that could be broken down and loaded in a car, truck or van. The sections can be any height and divided based on the types of tools and hardware required. The basic chest design is built the same no matter what your needs are; only the interior divisions are customized.

I designed the pull handle so it could swing over the lower (main) section for storage or transportation. Each box can be stacked on any other box, and you can assemble any combination of boxes to take along to the work site. The cover fits and latches to any section, so any combination of boxes that you decide to carry will have a latched top.

The ability to carry one section at a time is a real bonus. For years I've been lifting heavy tool chests into my vehicles, and my back has suffered the consequences. I don't know why I hadn't thought of the sectional tool chest concept before this. It's such a simple idea!

My tools are organized in their own sections. The heavy electric tools such as drills, jigsaws and sanders are in the bottom box. Hand tools are stored in another smaller top section, and the last section is dedicated to my hardware supplies for the particular project I'm working on. When I get to the project site, I simply take the sections apart and I'm ready to work without having to dig through a deep chest to sort my tools.

If you need tools and hardware on a job site, or do a lot of projects for family and friends, or just want a safe, secure and organized tool storage area, this is the project for you. I'm sure you'll enjoy building the mobile chest and custom designing the sections.

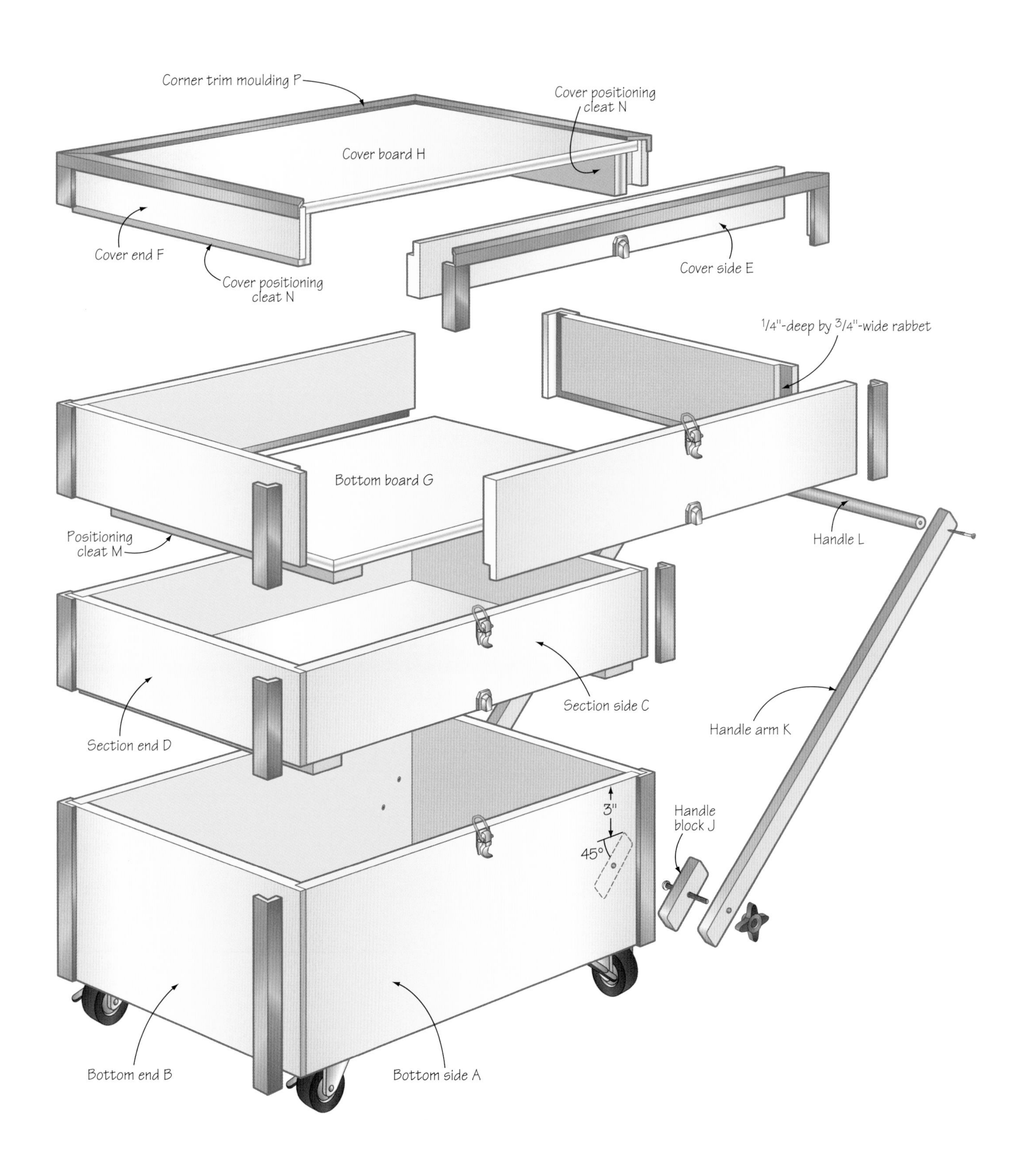
Corner trim moulding P
Cover positioning cleat N
Cover board H
Cover end F
Cover positioning cleat N
Cover side E
1/4"-deep by 3/4"-wide rabbet
Bottom board G
Positioning cleat M
Handle L
Section side C
Section end D
Handle arm K
3"
45°
Handle block J
Bottom end B
Bottom side A

inches (millimeters)

REFERENCE	QUANTITY	PART	STOCK	THICKNESS	(mm)	WIDTH	(mm)	LENGTH	(mm)
A	2	bottom sides	veneer ply	$^3/_4$	(19)	12	(305)	29	(737)
B	2	bottom ends	veneer ply	$^3/_4$	(19)	12	(305)	18	(457)
C	4	section sides	veneer ply	$^3/_4$	(19)	6	(152)	29	(737)
D	4	section ends	veneer ply	$^3/_4$	(19)	6	(152)	18	(457)
E	2	cover sides	veneer ply	$^3/_4$	(19)	3	(76)	29	(737)
F	2	cover ends	veneer ply	$^3/_4$	(19)	3	(76)	18	(457)
G	3	bottom boards	veneer ply	$^3/_4$	(19)	17	(432)	29	(737)
H	1	cover board	veneer ply	$^3/_4$	(19)	17	(432)	29	(737)
J	2	handle blocks	hardwood	$^3/_4$	(19)	$1^1/_2$	(38)	5	(127)
K	2	handle arms	hardwood	$^3/_4$	(19)	$13^9/_{16}$	(344)	30	(762)
L	1	handle	wood dowel	1	(25)			$20^1/_4$	(514)
M	4	positioning cleats	veneer ply	$^3/_4$	(19)	2	(51)	$16^1/_2$	(419)
N	2	cover position cleats	veneer ply	$^3/_4$	(19)	3	(76)	$16^1/_2$	(419)
P	1	corner trim moulding	hardwood	1	(25)	1	(25)	24'	(7315)

hardware & supplies

NOTE: QUANTITIES WILL VARY DEPENDING ON THE NUMBER OF CHEST SECTIONS BUILT.

	glue
	brad nails
	$1^1/_2$" (38mm) screws
	$1^1/_4$" (32mm) screws
16	$^1/_4$" x $1^1/_2$" (6mm x 38mm) carriage bolts with nuts
2	$^1/_4$" x 2" (6mm x 51mm) carriage bolts
2	handle-locking knobs
4	wheels/casters
8	chest handles
6	draw latches
2	decorative finishing washers

1 Cut the section panels A, B, C, D, E and F to the sizes indicated in the materials list. These panel dimensions are based on my stackable section sizes of a 12"-high base unit and two 6"-high top sections, as well as a chest cover. If you've decided on a different size configuration, please change the sizes before cutting the sheet material. Each of the B, D and F end panels needs a $3/4$"-wide by $1/4$"-deep rabbet on each end to receive the side panels. Use a stacked carbide dado blade, or router equipped with a $3/4$" bit, to form the rabbets.

2 Leave the dado blade set in the same position as in step 1. Cut a $3/4$"-wide by $1/4$"-deep rabbet on the inside face (same face as the previous rabbets) of all sides and end panels. These rabbets will receive the bottom and cover panels.

3 Assemble the four frames by securing the sides in the end rabbets with glue and $1\frac{1}{2}$"-long screws. Drill pilot holes for the screws to minimize material splits. The screw heads will be hidden by corner moulding. The rabbets on the long edges of the panels should be aligned to properly receive the bottom boards G.

4 The bottom boards G and cover board H are installed in the frame rabbets. Use glue and a few brad nails, driven through the face side, to secure these panels.

5 Attach the two handle blocks J. These blocks will allow the handle arms K to clear the corner moulding, which will be attached in a later step. Before securing the blocks on the base case, drill holes in the center of each one and install a 2"-long by 1⁄4"-diameter carriage bolt. You'll need to counterbore the bolt holes so the carriage bolt head is beneath the block surface. Use a sander to remove and round the handle block corners. The handle block will be installed at a 45° angle, 3" below the top edge and 1" in from the case end panel. Use glue and 1 1⁄4"-long screws, through the inside face of the bottom case sides, to attach the blocks.

6 Drill a 15⁄16"-diameter hole on one end of each handle arm K. The holes should be 1 1⁄4" in from each end and centered on the handle. Use a 3⁄8"-radius roundover bit in your router to soften the outside edges of both handle arms. These arms will be attached to the handle blocks using 1⁄4" threaded knobs, which are available at many home-improvement and hardware stores.

7 The handle L is a 1"-diameter wood dowel rod. Drill a 3⁄8"-deep by 1"-diameter hole on the inside face of each handle arm. Center the hole 3⁄4" below the top end on each arm. Install the handle in the arm holes and secure each end with a 1 1⁄4"-long screw and decorative finishing washer. Don't use glue on these joints, as you may want to dismantle the handle and arm assembly in the future. The handle arms, with handle attached, should fold over the opposite end of the bottom case to minimize space when transporting the chest.

8 I'm installing 3"-diameter wheels, which have a locking option, on my toolbox base section. The wheel base plates are set 1 1⁄2" in from each end edge. Use 1 1⁄2"-long by 1⁄4"-diameter carriage bolts to attach the wheels. My stackable toolbox will be used in my shop, on concrete floors in a garage or on paved driveways most of the time. However, if your chest will be used on rough or uneven surfaces, such as grass and unpaved driveways, you should consider installing larger-diameter wheels.

9 Cut the positioning cleats M to the size shown. They are aligned $\frac{3}{4}$" in from each section edge and secured with $1\frac{1}{4}$"-long screws. Don't glue these cleats, because not only do they align the sections when stacked, they also act as feet and may need replacing when worn.

10 The cover should also be fitted with the two positioning cleats N. Secure them to the inside face of each cover end panel using $1\frac{1}{4}$"-long screws. These cleats will position and align the cover on any of the stackable trays.

11 Attach draw latches on each stackable section. Be sure to align and secure each latch in the same position so any section, or cover, can be attached to different stack arrangements. This mix-and-match feature is handy, so take extra care when installing these latches.

12 I'm installing simple metal D-handles on all sections as well as the cover. These are medium-duty handles, but you can just as easily install heavy-duty chest handles if you plan to carry heavier loads in your chest.

13 The corner trim moulding P installed around the cover's top perimeter, as well as the trim on the chest section corners, is 1" corner moulding. This trim is available in all lumberyards. I'm using oak to contrast with the maple veneer, but any wood will be fine. If you plan to paint your chest, use inexpensive finger-jointed pine trim. Cut the pieces to size and attach them around the cover rim, as well as on the four vertical corners of each chest section, using glue and brad nails.

14 The interior spaces of each stackable section can be divided or left open based on your requirements. Customize the space in each section for tools and hardware.

construction NOTES

This mobile tool chest project has dozens of design options. I mentioned a few in the introduction and throughout the construction steps. However, the height, width and length of each stackable section are the most obvious changes that can be made.

You may not need 6"-deep stackables or a 12"-deep base. If that's the case, change the sizes to suit your needs. As previously mentioned, the width and type of terrain this unit will be pulled over will determine how wide and what style of wheels you should use. If you do a lot of deck building, I would suggest you widen the base and use large-diameter wheels for the rugged yards you'll most likely encounter.

I used 3/4" maple veneer plywood and oak trim for my project. The chest is finished with three coats of water-based polyurethane. However, I was going to use plywood and finger-jointed pine trim. In that case, I would finish the chest with two or three coats of latex paint. But as I was walking through my local sheet material supplier, I noticed a few sheets of veneered maple seconds for sale. They were less expensive than the regular plywood, so I saved a few dollars and had a smoother surface to finish. That's one of the benefits with this project, because you can use any 3/4"-thick plywood sheet material. So look around your area for a good buy on sheet stock.

Also as previously mentioned, consider the loads that will be carried in the chest sections. If you plan to carry heavy tools, use heavy-duty chest handles on the sections. Consider using 1 1/2" x 1 1/2" square boards for the handle arms and a 1 1/4"-diameter dowel rod if you will be pulling heavy loads over rough surfaces.

adjustable worktable

PROJECT

Woodworkers often work on many types of projects throughout the year. One week it will be a small craft or carving project, and the next one might be a bathroom cabinet. A high worktable is great when working on small projects, but that same table is almost useless when building a cabinet case.

You could build two benches, one high and the other low, but most of us don't have that kind of room available. Why not build a worktable that can be raised and lowered to suit each requirement? Well, if you do a wide range of large and small projects, this worktable may be your solution to achieving a proper, and comfortable, workbench height.

This adjustable worktable can be fixed at 24" or 40" high and everything in between at 1½" increments. It's strong, with a heavy top that's perfectly flat, and has a replaceable surface. You can, as I did, add a pullout tool tray for small hand tools.

The adjustable-height feature is a bonus in many custom cabinet shops. A fixed-height bench means you're either bending over to work on small carvings or reaching over your head to assemble large cabinets. Both situations can be very tiring and a strain on your back. Fixing the table height at a comfortable level for the project you're currently building will add a great deal of enjoyment and comfort for any woodworker.

The "sandwiched" top, using ¾" particleboard, is heavy, so if you don't have someone to help change the table's height, I'll show you how to safely adjust it by yourself. The particleboard top, low-cost pine 2×4s, a few screws, hardware and glue make this an affordable project in the $150 to $200 range, depending on the cost of materials in your area.

Before starting, look at the scissor jack lift option at the end of this chapter. If you plan to change the height frequently, this system might be right for you. The scissor jack should be purchased first, as its dimensions might determine rail positions for your bench.

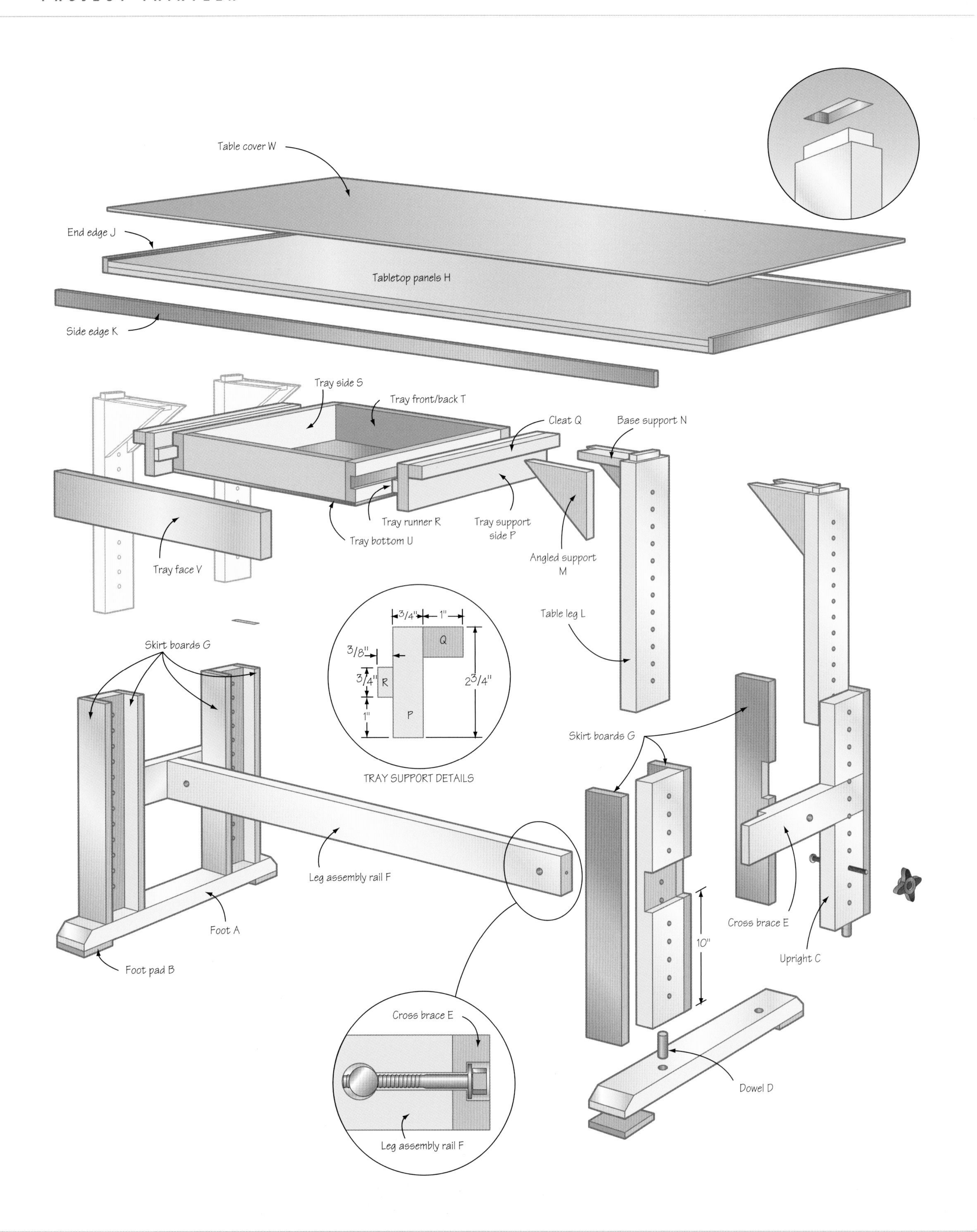
Table cover W
End edge J
Tabletop panels H
Side edge K
Tray side S
Tray front/back T
Cleat Q
Base support N
Tray runner R
Tray support side P
Tray bottom U
Angled support M
Tray face V
Table leg L
Skirt boards G
3/4"
1"
3/8"
3/4"
1"
Q
R
P
2 3/4"
TRAY SUPPORT DETAILS
Skirt boards G
Leg assembly rail F
Foot A
Foot pad B
10"
Cross brace E
Upright C
Cross brace E
Leg assembly rail F
Dowel D

inches (millimeters)

REFERENCE	QUANTITY	PART	STOCK	THICKNESS	(mm)	WIDTH	(mm)	LENGTH	(mm)
A	2	feet	solid wood	1⁵⁄₈	(41)	3¹⁄₂	(89)	28	(711)
B	4	foot pads	plywood	¹⁄₂	(13)	3¹⁄₂	(89)	3¹⁄₂	(89)
C	4	uprights	solid wood	1⁵⁄₈	(41)	3¹⁄₂	(89)	20	(508)
D	4	dowels	solid wood	1 dia.	(25)			3	(76)
E	2	cross braces	solid wood	1⁵⁄₈	(41)	3¹⁄₂	(89)	21	(533)
F	1	leg assembly rail	solid wood	1⁵⁄₈	(41)	3¹⁄₂	(89)	55	(1397)
G	8	skirt boards	solid wood	³⁄₄	(19)	3¹⁄₂	(89)	20	(508)
H	2	tabletop panels	particleboard	³⁄₄	(19)	27	(686)	72	(1829)
J	2	end edges	solid wood	³⁄₄	(19)	1³⁄₄	(45)	27	(686)
K	2	side edges	solid wood	³⁄₄	(19)	1³⁄₄	(45)	73¹⁄₂	(1867)
L	4	table legs	solid wood	1⁵⁄₈	(41)	3¹⁄₂	(89)	20³⁄₄	(527)
M	8	angled supports	particleboard	³⁄₄	(19)	6¹⁄₂	(165)	6¹⁄₂	(165)
N	4	base supports	particleboard	³⁄₄	(19)	2	(51)	5¹⁄₂	(140)
P	2	tray support sides	particleboard	³⁄₄	(19)	2³⁄₄	(70)	18	(457)
Q	2	cleats	hardwood	³⁄₄	(19)	1	(25)	18	(457)
R	2	tray runners	hardwood	³⁄₈	(10)	³⁄₄	(19)	18	(457)
S	2	tray sides	particleboard	³⁄₄	(19)	2¹⁄₄	(57)	18	(457)
T	2	tray front & back	particleboard	³⁄₄	(19)	2¹⁄₄	(57)	22¹⁄₂	(572)
U	1	tray bottom	plywood	¹⁄₄	(6)	18	(457)	22	(559)
V	1	tray face	solid wood	³⁄₄	(19)	3¹⁄₂	(89)	28	(711)
W	1	table cover	hardboard	¹⁄₄	(6)	27	(686)	72	(1829)

hardware & supplies

	1¹⁄₄" (32mm) screws
	1¹⁄₂" (38mm) screws
	2" (51mm) screws
	3" (76mm) screws
	brad nails
	small nails or double-sided tape
	glue
2	³⁄₈" x 5" (10mm x 127mm) bolts, nuts and washers
8	¹⁄₄" x 4" (6mm x 102mm) carriage bolts
8	fender washers
8	¹⁄₄" (6mm) diameter threaded knobs

1 Cut the two feet A to the size shown in the materials list. Both ends of each foot can be mitered with a 45° cut on the top face, 1" back from the ends. This technique adds visual interest to the legs and removes any sharp corners.

2 The two feet should have foot pads B installed at both ends. They can be changed as they wear or are damaged but, more importantly, will help to stabilize the table on rough floors. Attach each pad with two $1\frac{1}{2}$" long screws, but don't use glue here.

3 The four uprights C require a dado starting 10" above the bottom end. These dadoes are $\frac{13}{16}$" deep (or half the thickness of the material used) and $3\frac{1}{2}$" wide. Cut the dadoes with a stacked dado head cutter on your table saw. Or, see the shop tip that explains how to cut these dadoes using a standard blade on your table saw or circular saw.

SHOP *tip*

You can cut dadoes using a standard blade on your table saw or with a circular saw. First, make a series of kerf cuts, about $\frac{1}{4}$" apart, along the dado width. Next, use a hammer and sharp chisel to clean the waste from the cut.

4 The uprights C are positioned 3½" from each foot end. Draw a line from corner to corner on the bottom end of each upright to determine the center point. Trace the upright outline and position on the feet, holding the back face of each upright flush with the back or outside edge of each foot. Draw lines on the traced rectangles to determine their center points.

5 At this point you can drill a 1"-diameter hole at the marked center point of each foot and upright. However, it's difficult to drill straight holes by hand in separate pieces to be joined. I suggest that you attach the uprights to the feet using glue and two 3"-long screws through the bottom face of the feet and into the uprights. These screws will hold the upright-to-foot connection while we proceed with the next step.

6 Drill a 1"-diameter hole, 3" deep, through the foot and into the upright end. Try to hold the drill as straight as possible. Drive a 1"-diameter by 3"-long wood dowel D into the hole. Apply glue to the dowels before driving them into the holes.

7 Cut the two cross braces E to size. Form a 13⁄16"-deep by 3½"- wide rabbet on each end. The cross braces fit between the uprights and are secured in the dadoes with glue and two 1¼" long screws.

8 The leg assembly rail F joins the two leg assemblies by attaching to the cross braces. Drill a 1½"-diameter hole 3½" from each leg rail end. Be sure to center the holes on the 3½"-wide face of the rail. Clamp the rail between the two leg assemblies flush with the top edges of the cross braces and centered 10½"from each end. Carefully drill ⅜"-diameter holes through the cross braces into the leg rail center. The holes should exit on one edge of the 1½"-diameter holes in the leg rail. Use ⅜"-diameter by 5"-long bolts with nuts and washers to secure the leg rail to each of the leg assemblies.

9 Once the bolts are tight and the leg rail is secured to the cross braces, drive two 3" long wood screws into each end above and below the bolts. These will not add a great deal of holding power as they are driven into leg rail end grain, but will act as pins to stop the rail from twisting. Don't use glue on these connections, so the table can be dismantled for moving.

10 Each upright will have two skirt boards. These skirts will form a channel for the tabletop legs and help to stabilize the table in its various adjusted positions. Cut the eight skirt boards G and attach them to the uprights with glue and 1½"-long screws. Install the outside skirt boards first because the inner skirts require a notch to fit around the cross braces.

11 The remaining four inside skirt boards require a notch, as discussed in the previous step. The notch is 1⅝"deep by 3½" wide and aligned, beginning 10" from the bottom edge, to the cross braces. Notch the boards on a table saw with a dado blade or use the procedure described in the next shop tip.

SHOP *tip*

As you can see in the photograph for step 11, I have gang clamped the boards together for the notch cut. This technique should be used when cutting a number of boards to ensure they are all the same. It also reduces the amount of passes that have to be made on the saw.

If you don't have a table saw, use a jigsaw to cut the notches. A band saw can also be used, or they can be cut by hand.

12 Install the inside skirt boards, using glue and three 1½" long screws.

13 Put the base aside for now and cut the two ¾"-thick tabletop panels H, which measure 27" wide by 72" long. I'm using ¾"-thick particleboard, but any sheet material can be used to build the top. Glue the two sheets together. Be sure they are accurately aligned to each other and clamp tightly until the adhesive sets up. You might also want to add some weight in the middle to ensure a good bond.

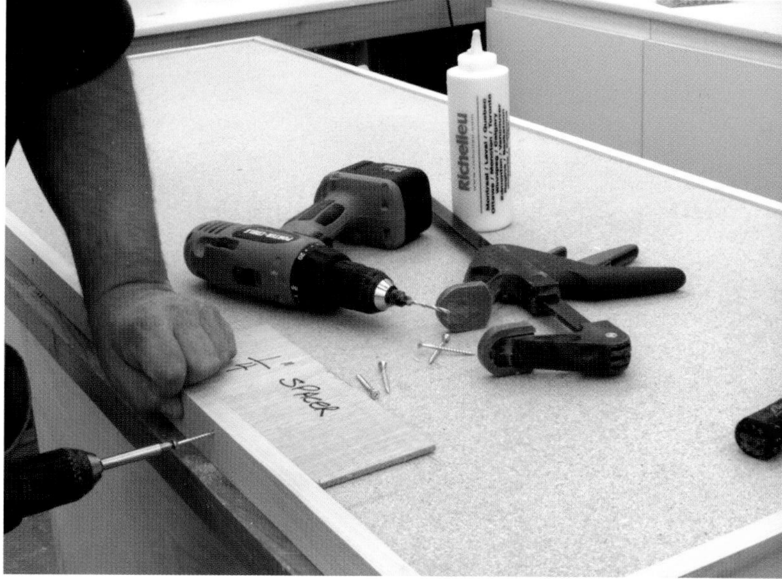

14 The edges of the sheet material are banded with ¾"-thick wood. I will be adding a ¼"-thick hardboard (called tempered or Masonite board) as a replaceable top, so the wood used to edge the top will be 1¾" high. The wood edges J and K can be attached with biscuits, screws in counterbored holes filled with plugs, or screws with the heads flush to the edge surface. Pick a method that suits you, but use glue as part of the fastening system. Cut the edges J and K. Attach the strips ¼" above the table top surface using a guide that's the same thickness as the top material.

15 Turn the tabletop upside down and center the base on the top. Trace the inside perimeter of the uprights and skirt boards on the underside of the top. These lines will indicate where the table legs will be positioned.

16 Next, use a scrap piece of 1⅝" x 3½" stock to trace the final line for the leg positions.

17 Cut the four table legs L to the size indicated on the materials list. They are the same size as the base uprights with an added ¾", which will be used for a tenon on one end. Use a stacked dado cutter on your table saw, or a standard blade, to cut a ¼" deep by ¾"-wide rabbet on all four faces of each leg. Those cuts will form a tenon that's 1⅛" wide by 3" long on one end of the four legs.

18 Use the leg outlines that were previously drawn to mark the mortise position. Draw lines ¼" inside the rectangles to define the cut lines for the four mortises. Use a flat-bottomed drill bit (1" in diameter) to remove most of the waste. Each mortise is ¾" deep, so mark the drill depth position on your bit. Use a sharp chisel to remove the remaining waste. The finished mortises should be ¾"deep by 1⅛" wide by 3" long.

19 Before applying glue to the leg tenons, build the four support brackets. They are made with two pieces of angled supports M cut at 45°, and a base support N that spans the two angled supports. Cut parts M and N, then use glue with 2"-long screws to assemble the leg braces.

20 Use glue and 3"-long screws to attach the brackets to the legs. The base supports N will rest on the tabletop, so align the bracket with the top end of the tenon.

21 Apply glue to the leg tenons and bracket bottoms. Use 2"-long screws through the base support N to secure the legs to the table.

SHOP *tip*

If the uprights and skirts don't slide easily over the legs, apply a coat of floor paste wax to the legs. The base will then slide easily as long as you accurately traced the positions and cut the mortises correctly.

22 Place the base assembly on the table, sliding the skirts over the legs. Drill ¼"-diameter holes through the uprights and legs. Make a template with holes spaced 1¼" on center beginning 1" from the bottom of the uprights and end 1" above the tabletop.

23 The lower section is attached to the upper section with ¼"-diameter by 4"-long carriage bolts, a large fender washer, and a threaded knob. All the hardware is available at most home centers. Each leg/upright has two bolt assemblies that are located in different holes as the table height is adjusted.

24 The tool tray case and support assembly can be built with sheet material left over after cutting the tabletop panels. My tool tray is 18" deep by 24" wide and 3½" high. The tray support sides P are 2¾"high with a 1"-wide cleat Q on the outside face and a ⅜"-thick by ¾"-high tray runner R on the inside face. The tray runners begin 1" above the bottom edge of sides P and are secured with glue and brad nails. Set the two support sides 1½" behind the table edge. Secure both assemblies with glue and 2" screws so the tray will be centered on the table. The inside dimension, or inside support side face to inside support side face, must be 24¹⁄₁₆" to accommodate the tool tray case.

26 Cut a ¹³⁄₁₆"-wide by ⅜"-deep groove along each side of the tool tray. The groove begins 1" above the tray's bottom. Use a stacked dado cutter on your table saw or a router bit to cut the groove.

25 Assemble the tool tray using parts S, T and U. The corners are joined with simple butt joints, glue and 2"-long screws. The tray box sides S require a ¹³⁄₁₆"-wide groove that's ⅜" deep to slide on the runners R. Be sure to locate the screws as close to the top and bottom as possible so they won't be in the groove path. Attach the ¼" plywood bottom U using glue and brad nails.

27 The tray face V is a piece of ¾" solid wood. It's wide enough to cover the support assembles and act as a stop. Align the face with the tool tray centered from side to side and ¼" higher than the tray's top edge. Use three 1¼" long screws, through the back face of the front tray board, to secure the face. The amount of material hanging below the tray can be used as a handle.

28 The table cover W is ¼"-thick hardboard. It can be attached to the table with small nails or double-sided tape. When necessary, the cover can be reversed or replaced, so don't use any adhesive when installing the cover.

Adjusting the Table Height Manually

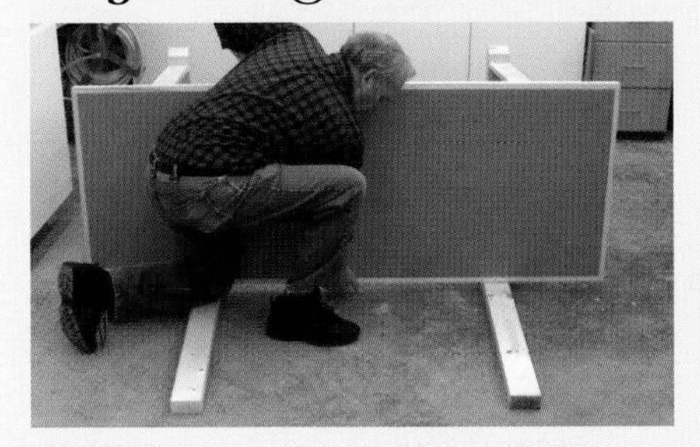

STEP 1 Adjusting the table height with two people is relatively easy. However, if you work alone as I do most of the time, you'll need an easy way to change the height. I first remove the tool tray, then lay two 2x4s on the floor. The table can be tipped to rest on the 2x4s.

STEP 2 Tip the table on its top and adjust the legs to any height you require. Once the bolts are in place, turn the table right-side up.

Adjusting the Table Height Mechanically

STEP 1 A scissor jack that can travel 16" vertically is used to adjust the table in an upright position. Purchase a jack that has a travel of 16", not one that has a maximum height of 16". Maximum- height dimensions given for scissor jacks include the height of the jack at rest. The fully closed scissor uses 4" to 5" of space and reduces the travel distance. The best way to check jack travel is to measure the top plate at rest, then crank it all the way up and measure the top plate's position. The difference should be at least 16". The jack should be located at the center of the table, measuring from side to side and front to back, for balanced lifting. Attach a plywood platform, a little larger than the scissor jack's footprint to the leg rail assembly. Use as many pieces of wood as required so the jack sits on the platform with its top plate touching the underside of the table when both (jack and worktable) are in the lowest position. The platform can be anchored with screws, and the scissor jack's base can be screwed to the platform. You may have to drill holes in the jack's metal foot for the screws.

STEP 2 Remove the bolts and knobs in the legs and turn the jack handle until the desired height is reached. Replace the bolts in their new holes and lock the table. Scissor jacks with a minimum of 16" travel are often available at auto supply stores, but they can be found at all recreational vehicle (RV) accessory stores. These jacks are commonly used to level RV trailers when parked. Installing the jack will affect drawer design and depth, so take that issue into consideration before building the drawer. This option may not be necessary for everyone, and the cost ($75 to $100) for a good scissor jack might make you reconsider this option, but if you need frequent height changes, it's well worth the money spent.

construction NOTES

I used furniture-grade pine for my uprights and legs. The tabletop was made with two layers of 3/4"-thick particleboard. However, any 2x4 stock and sheet material can be substituted; it's your choice.

Particleboard sheet material is heavy and stable. The weight is a bonus because it keeps the table well anchored but does create problems when the table height has to be adjusted. However, I prefer a heavier table, and if I use the height changing method as shown, it's not too much of an inconvenience.

My tool tray is shallow because I plan to store chisels and rulers for easy access. You can easily change the depth and width to suit your needs as long as the depth isn't greater than the leg-rail-to-tabletop space when the table is fully lowered. You can also make two trays or drawers, using the same construction steps, by adding two tray runner supports.

The table height adjustment range is from 24" to 40". That should be suitable for most woodworking tasks but can be changed if you have special requirements. Remember, the height of the uprights, tabletop thickness, and foot assembly height determine the lowest tabletop height, so take those dimensions into consideration when designing your worktable.

Finally, you may need a wider or longer table. If so, change the tabletop panel dimensions as well as the leg rail length. Remember the rule of 12s for your bench. Should you want to sit at the worktable, use a chair or stool height that's 12" lower than the tabletop surface for comfortable seating.

SUPPLIERS

There have been many suppliers who have contributed products, material and technical support during the project building phase.

I appreciate how helpful they've been and recommend the companies without hesitation.

If you have trouble locating a product that I've mentioned, please email me at danny@cabinetmaking.com.

ADAMS & KENNEDY — THE WOOD SOURCE
6178 Mitch Owen Road
P.O. Box 700
Manotick, Ontario, Canada K4M 1A6
613-822-6800
www.wood-source.com
Wood supply

ADJUSTABLE CLAMP COMPANY
417 North Ashland Avenue
Chicago, Illinois 60622
312-666-0640
www.adjustableclamp.com
Clamps

DELTA MACHINERY
4825 Highway 45 North
P.O. Box 2468
Jackson, Tennessee 38302-2468
800-223-7278 (U.S.)
800-463-3582 (Canada)
www.deltawoodworking.com
Woodworking tools

EXAKTOR PRECISION WOODWORKING TOOLS, INC.
136 Watline #1 & 2
Mississauga, Ontario, Canada L4C 2E2
800-387-9789
www.exaktortools.com
Accessories for the table saw

GENERAL & GENERAL INTERNATIONAL
8360 du Champ-D'eau
Montreal, Quebec, Canada H1P 1Y3
514-326-1161
www.general.ca
Woodworking machinery

HOUSE OF TOOLS
100 Mayfield Common Northwest
Edmonton, Alberta, Canada T5P 4B3
800-661-3987
www.houseoftools.com
Woodworking tools and hardware

JESSEM TOOL COMPANY
124 Big Bay Point Road
Barrie, Ontario, Canada L4N 9B4
866-272-7492
www.jessem.com
Rout-R-Slide and Rout-R-Lift

LANGEVIN & FOREST
9995 Boulevard Pie IX
Montreal, Quebec, Canada H1Z 3X1
800-889-2060
www.langevinforest.com
Tools, wood and books

LEE VALLEY TOOLS LTD.
P.O. Box 1780
Ogdensburg, New York 13669-6780
800-267-8735
www.leevalley.com
Fine woodworking tools and hardware

PORTER-CABLE CORPORATION
4825 Highway 45 North
P.O. Box 2468
Jackson, Tennessee 38302-2468
800-487-8665
www.porter-cable.com
Woodworking tools

RICHELIEU HARDWARE
7900, West Henri-Bourassa
Ville St-Laurent, Quebec, Canada H4S 1V4
800-619-5446 (U.S.)
800-361-6000 (Canada)
www.richelieu.com
Hardware supplies

ROCKLER WOODWORKING AND HARDWARE
4365 Willow Drive
Medina, Minnesota 55340
800-279-4441
www.rockler.com
Woodworking tools and hardware

TOOL TREND LTD.
140 Snow Boulevard
Concord, Ontario, Canada L4K 4C1
416-663-8665
Woodworking tools and hardware

VAUGHAN
11414 Maple Avenue
Hebron, Illinois 60034
815-648-2446
www.vaughanmfg.com
Hammers and other tools

WOLFCRAFT NORTH AMERICA
333 Swift Road
Addison, Illinois 60101-1448
630-773-4777
www.wolfcraft.com
Woodworking hardware and accessories

WOODCRAFT
P.O. Box 1686
Parkersburg, West Virginia 26102-1686
800-225-1153
www.woodcraft.com
Woodworking hardware and accessories

WOODWORKER'S HARDWARE
P.O. Box 180
Sauk Rapids, Minnesota 56379-0180
800-383-0130
www.wwhardware.com
Woodworking tools and accessories; finishing supplies; books and plans

Plywood and particleboard material information and suppliers can be found at the Panolam or Uniboard sites www.panolam.com and www.uniboard.com.

INDEX

A
Adjustable Worktable, 114-125

B
Base Cabinet Work Center, 74-83

C
Carpenter's Toolbox, 84-95
Carver's Tool Chest, 96-105
Circular saws
  cutting dadoes and rabbets with, 18, 118
Crosscutting panel jig, 73

D
Dadoes
  circular saw, cutting with, 18, 118
Drawer faces, 81

F
Fingerjoint jig, 95
Fold-away Work Center, 22-31

H
Hand Tool Wall Cabinet, 66-73
Hanger bolts and knobs, 20

I
Introduction, 6

J
Jigs
  crosscutting panel jig, 73
  fingerjoint jig, 95
Joints
  celebrating vs. hiding, 12

M
Materials lists
  Adjustable Worktable, 117
  Base Cabinet Work Center, 77
  Carpenter's Toolbox, 87
  Carver's Tool Chest, 99
  Fold-away Work Center, 25
  Hand Tool Wall Cabinet, 69
  Mobile Tool Chest, 109
  Rolling Shop Cart, 63
  Rolling Tool Cabinet, 35
  Simple Sawhorses, 55
  Simple Workbench, 17
  Tall Storage Cabinets, 47
  Toolbox Tote, 11
Medium-density fiberboard
  screws, driving, 26, 49
Mobile Tool Chest, 106-113

P
Projects
  Adjustable Worktable, 114-125
  Base Cabinet Work Center, 74-83
  Carpenter's Toolbox, 84-95
  Carver's Tool Chest, 96-105
  Fold-away Work Center, 22-31
  Hand Tool Wall Cabinet, 66-73
  Mobile Tool Chest, 106-113
  Rolling Shop Cart, 60-65
  Rolling Tool Cabinet, 32-43
  Simple Sawhorses, 52-59
  Simple Workbench, 14-21
  Tall Storage Cabinets, 44-51
  Toolbox Tote, 8-13

R
Rabbets
  circular saw, cutting with, 18
Rolling Shop Cart, 60-65
Rolling Tool Cabinet, 32-43

S
Simple Sawhorses, 52-59
Simple Workbench, 14-21
Splitting
  medium-density fiberboard, 26, 49
Suppliers, 126-127

T
Tall Storage Cabinets, 44-51
Toolbox Tote, 8-13

W
Wood edge tapes, 69